MW01062086

Basketball's Box Offense

Herb Brown

MASTERS PRESS

A division of Howard W. Sams & Co.

Masters Press (A Division of Howard W. Sams & Co.)
2647 Waterfront Parkway, East Drive, Suite 300
Indianapolis, IN 46214

Library of Congress Cataloging-in-Publication Data

Brown, Herb, 1936-
Basketball's box offense / by Herb Brown.
      p. cm.
    ISBN: 1-57028-031-2: $12.95
    1. Basketball – Offense.   I. Title.

GV889.B76 1995
796.323'2 – dc20   95-12477
                                           CIP

98 99 00 01   10 9 8 7 6 5 4 3

Foreword

There are those of us who coach, no matter what level, who sincerely enjoy our work and feel that coaching is a labor of love. Then there are those who coach because it was the job that was available, a way to get recognition, make money or gain power. The real coach is one who works because he or she is a professional and believes in the position of a coach.

Herb Brown is one of these "real" coaches. He has paid his dues many times over and will continue to do so because he believes in what he does. A close look at a Herb Brown resume tells the whole story.

Part of that story is found in these pages. The contents of this book are for you ... an attempt by Herb to give back to a profession and the game he dearly respects.

You can be sure that anything written in this book has worked for Herb and the hope is that what's found on these pages will stimulate your thinking or penetrate your philosophy. If so, Herb Brown has been successful — again.

Good luck.

Bob Hill, head coach, San Antonio Spurs

Credits:
Cover design by Suzanne Lincoln
Illustration reproduction by Phil Velikan
Edited by Kim Heusel
Editorial assistance by Holly Kondras
Text layout by Kim Heusel

Cover Photos © Frank Howard

Acknowledgments

I've had the good fortune to coach with and against some of the world's outstanding coaches in the National Basketball Association, Continental Basketball Association, Western Basketball Association, in Puerto Rico, Europe, and on the college level in the United States. I have admired them, studied their techniques and watched their teams play.

Although they might not personally realize it, some of my mentors have been Red Auerbach, Bobby Knight, Dean Smith, Red Holtzman, Tommy Heinsohn, Jack Ramsey, Butch Van Bredakoff and Lou Carnesecca. I also have profited over the years from discussions with Del Harris, Bob Hill, Phil Jackson, John MacLeod, John Wetzel, Rick Barry, Al Bianchi, Max Zaslofsky, Jerry Colangelo, Tex Winter, Jim Cleamons, Jack McKinney, Jerry Krause, Ray Paterson, George Karl, Donnie Walsh and Larry Brown.

I've been blessed with some great assistant coaches and respected basketball associates, some of whom may not be well-known, but who helped me immeasurably. They not only contributed to the success of our teams but are responsible for a great deal of what I have been able to accomplish. I'll always treasure the contributions of Ed Krinsky, Bill Ficke, Phil Robinson, Larry Jones, Eddie Miller, Humberto Ramirez, Frank Tirico, Len Ginsberg, Adrian Smith, Ed Visscher, Gary Walters, Al Baldini, Jim Valvano, Frank Gugliotta Sr., Roy Rubin, Paco Garcia, Pete Haubner, Henry Dickerson, Ron Rutledge, Al Menendez, Miguel Nolis, Roger Brown, Herb Machol, Fuzzy Levane, Walter Szcerbiak, Roger Morningstar of Converse, and Gar Heard and Billy King of the Indiana Pacers.

Special thanks to Roy Ilowit, George Kaftan, Bill Davidson, Oscar Feldman and Haskell Cohen who believed in me and gave me my first opportunities on the college and professional basketball levels, and also to Tony Roberts, Sonny Simon and Gerry Wolken for their support and unyielding encouragement; also to Holly Kondras, Kim Heusel and all of the people at Masters Press who helped make this book a reality.

Much of a coach's success is due to the outstanding players he has coached. Many my former players have gone on to outstanding careers in coaching and other professions. I can't thank each of them individually, but I'll continue to have fond memories of the dedicated players from C.W. Post College, State University of New York at Stony Brook; Canovanas, Isabela, Carolina, Ponce and Guaynabo of Puerto Rico; the Puerto Rico Coquis and Cincinnati Slammers of the CBA; the Israel Sabras; the Tuscon Gunners of the WBA; Taugres, Joventud and Zaragoza of Spain; and the NBA's Detroit Pistons, Houston Rockets, Chicago Bulls, Phoenix Suns, and especially the Indiana Pacers players, staff and everyone connected with the organization who have made 1995-96 such a great experience. Everyone connected with those teams was a winner and will forever be a part of my life.

To Cindy, my wife, best friend, inspiration and constant companion these last 12 years.

Table of Contents

Introduction

Writing a book about basketball has always been one of my ambitions, not only because coaching is my profession and I truly love and enjoy my work, but because reading has been one of my hobbies. Beginning with my fascination with Clair Bee's Chip Hilton books, I have tried to read every biography about coaches in every sport as well as every book about coaching basketball. The first basketball coaching book I ever read was *Basketball for the Player, the Fan and the Coach* by Arnold "Red" Auerbach. It still occupies a prominent place on my desk.

The enjoyment and knowledge gained from reading about other coaches' ideas and experiences has been integrated into my own coaching philosophy and style. This book is the result of what I have learned from reading their articles and books, observing their practices, and exchanging ideas with them at clinics and camps. I marvel at their resiliency.

I chose to write about offensive basketball because, as any of my former players and opponents can tell you, I've always taught and preached defense. My teams are capable of defending and stopping anyone, but as a realist, I know that the team scoring the most points wins.

As a coach, I have had the opportunity to travel throughout the United States and to many parts of the world. One thing is clear: Basketball is universal and competitive no matter where and at what level it's played. Americans have not cornered the market on innovation and new ideas, but we have helped make basketball an international pastime and arguably the most popular sport in the world.

Herb Brown

Symbols Used in Our Diagrams

Offensive Players:	**1, 2, 3, 4, 5**
Defensive Players:	**X1, X2, X3, X4, X5**
Player with the Ball:	(1) (Player's number is circled)
Path of Player without the Ball:	⟶
Path and Direction of the Pass:	– – – – – – – ⟶
Optional Pass:	– – – –⊙– – – ⟶
Path and Direction of Player Dribbling the Ball:	⟿
Player Screening and Then Cutting:	
Entry Pass:	– – – – – – – ⟶
Player Cutting and Pivoting:	
Player Setting a Screen:	

Key to Diagrams Found in this Book

1. Pass: *Dotted line with an arrow at the end to show direction.*

(1)

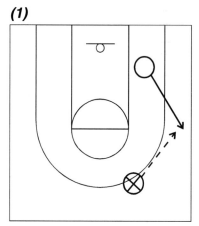

3. Pass and cut with return pass: *Number of slashes in the dotted line shows the number of the progression of the pass in this diagram. An optional pass would have a small circle above the dotted line.*

(3)

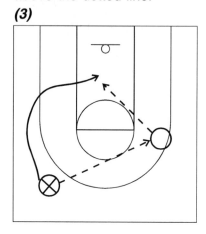

(2)

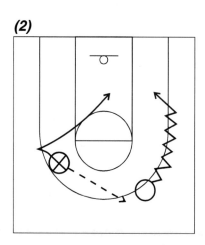

2. Player cut: *Unbroken line with an arrow at the end.* **Dribble:** *Jagged line with an arrow at the end.*

(4)

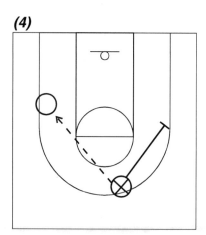

4. *Screen away after you make a pass.*

Key to Diagrams Found in this Book

1. *Player setting a screen:* *Unbroken line with an arrow and a smaller line at its end to show the screen.*

(1)

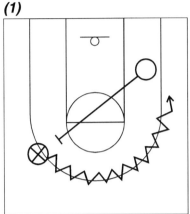

3. *Circle or curl offensive cut:* *Unbroken curved line with an arrow at the end to indicate direction.*

(3)

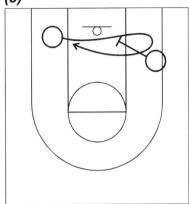

2. *Player setting a screen and then rolling to the basket.*

(2)

4. *Screen across and pivot back to the ball in the direction opposite that of the cutter*

(4)

5. *"V" cut with flare move away.*

(5)

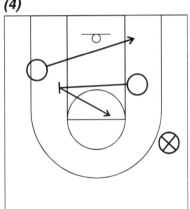

1

Introduction to the Box Offense

The Philosophy of the Offense

Scoring quickly and easily by putting maximum pressure on the defense is the philosophy behind the box offense. Once a team gains possession of the ball, it must try to create immediate scoring opportunities by penetrating. A team's ability to penetrate the opposing defense is the key to winning.

Keeping this in mind, a major emphasis is placed on grabbing offensive as well as defensive rebounds. Players must anticipate missed shots and should be expected to rebound aggressively by always blocking or boxing out, establishing rebounding triangles, covering the weakside backboard, trying to capture long rebounds and crashing the boards from the outside. Slapping loose rebounds to teammates or pre-determined corners or areas of the court where the ball can be recovered can also set up immediate fast break opportunities.

When possession is obtained after a rebound, steal, deflection, turnover or other violation, push the ball upcourt as quickly as possible. The defense may be caught napping which provides another quick scoring opportunity.

The objective of moving the defense and fast-breaking a full 94 feet whenever possible is best accomplished by rapidly passing the ball up the court to the free man. This not only rewards him for hustling back and getting free, but provides an opportunity to penetrate to the basket for a shot or at least a foul and trip to the free-throw line.

First try to score by utilizing either the middle or sideline fast break theory. Then use the transition attack, secondary or early offense, the half-court or set offense, or the motion or passing game. Always try to score quickly against all types of pressure, combination and zone defenses. You want to score rapidly before opponents can organize or establish a defense. The objective is to force the fast break, but **not force the shot.** Take high-percentage shots, not poor ones.

Prepare your team to try to score on nearly every out-of-bounds opportunity, and from defensive and offensive free-throw situations. The objective is to keep relentless pressure on the defense.

In transition or fast-break situations, quick outlet passes, long ones if possible, cover as much distance as possible in the shortest period of time. The fewer dribbles, the faster the fast break. Encourage your players to execute quickly and efficiently to help them develop their individual offensive skills. Implore them to be unselfish, get the ball to the free man and let the game come to them. Each player will eventually have opportunities to score because of the multiple aspects of the offense and the number of options constantly being run.

Coach's Edge

In real estate, timing and location normally dictate whether or not you make a sale. When you add proper spacing to this equation you have the formula for winning offensive basketball.

Both middle and sideline fast breaks include turnouts, curls, flares, crossing, diagonal screening, upblocks, downscreens and other offensive maneuvers. Covering the length of the court as quickly as possible puts maximum pressure on the defense. The first big man downcourt goes to the ballside low post block, the wing men cross and the last man down (normally the second big man) becomes the trailer or center fielder. It's his responsibility to reverse the ball and make the offense move and react, which creates additional scoring opportunities when players go the full length of the court and attack using the in, out and over principle: First pass and look inside to score. If this is not possible, pass outside and over in an effort to move the defense and create other scoring opportunities before the defense can react.

If no transition or fast-break opportunities are available or if it was previously decided to run a specific play you then set up and try to score by using your set offense. You may decide to do this because a change of tempo is needed, it is a special situation that requires an immediate basket, or a change in the opponent's defense has been spotted. In this situation, players need to read the defense and take advantage of what the other team gives them. Don't stop looking for "opportunity" or "rhythm and range" scoring attempts. Always try to penetrate and score, or penetrate and pitch by moving the basketball in, out and over. Swinging the basketball from side to side effectively breaks the defense down by attacking it from many different angles.

Patience is another key ingredient in the attack. Players must be cognizant of their teammates' strengths since the offense is designed to maximize the abilities of both the team and each individual.

Know when to attack methodically and when to hurry. Have predetermined signals to know when the shot or game clock is running down. Players should know when to shoot and also know the difference between a good and a bad shot. To be successful, players must also know the shooting tendencies and abilities of their teammates. This is a tremendous advantage in offensive rebounding because teammates' shots can be anticipated and you will have a good idea of where the rebound will bounce. The offense must provide defensive balance and rebounding position to be effective. It's inherent in a good offense that it have the **floor balance to make the immediate transition from offense to defense.**

Never overlook the importance of taking care of the basketball. It's a precious commodity, and the team that controls it usually wins. **Turnovers are a part of the game but the team with the least amount has a big edge.**

Coach's Edge

Your players should know not to cross the mid-court line and immediately stop with the ball when being pressured. This enables the defense to use the 10-second (mid-court) line and possibly the nearest sideline as additional defenders. Crosscourt passes should not be attempted against pressure in this situation. If the ball is stolen here it nearly always results in an easy two points for your opponents.

Coach's Edge

When talking to your players about protecting the basketball, emphasize using the first pass to get the ball in play and the second to break the pressure against pressing defenses. It's imperative that your receivers work extra hard to establish passing lanes when getting free.

Elements of Basketball's Box Offense

The half-court box offense has many advantages. It's easily taught and is effective at all levels of basketball. It's not only multiple and flexible, it can be adapted to individual coaching philosophies and teaching techniques. I have coached against this offense and have seen it used successfully in the United States, Europe and South America. Many NBA teams, including the New York Knicks, Milwaukee Bucks and Phoenix Suns, used it against my Detroit Pistons teams and many NBA teams are still using it today.

Internationally, championship teams in Yugoslavia, Russia, Spain, Italy, France and Greece depend on it, and many NBA coaches have used it while coaching in Puerto Rico, including Red Holtzman, Jack Ramsey, Phil Jackson, K.C. Jones, Bernie Bickerstaff and Del Harris. Seattle coach George Karl used it against my teams in Spain when he coached Real Madrid and when I was coaching Taugres and Joventud.

It incorporates many elements of John Wooden's revered UCLA offense and provides the structure and flexibility to work well at the college and high school levels for men's or women's teams. It's not only fundamentally sound, it's functional.

The following points are useful in helping determine if this type of offensive system can meet your specific coaching needs:

- It provides rapid entry from your transition or early offense.

- It easily defines the areas on the court for effective spacing. The ideal space between players for the box offense is 15 to 20 feet, but this varies with the level of basketball — professional, college or high school.

- It gives your primary ball handler or point guard the necessary latitude to be creative. All great offenses permit exceptional penetrating possibilities. This offense is no exception.

- Each position on the floor is almost interchangeable, placing additional pressure on individual defensive players.

- Coaches can utilize the individual abilities of new players each season.

- It provides outstanding angles for delivering the ball to players in every scoring area of the floor.

- It establishes great offensive and defensive floor balance and position.

- Your team has great offensive rebounding coverage.

- Each player's position and his responsibility are easily defined.

- It has options for relieving any defensive pressure your team might face.

- It utilizes all offensive techniques, screens and cuts.

- It creates many misdirection opportunities on offense.

- It adapts easily to other offensive sets: 1-4 high or low, 1-2-2, and double stack.

- It presents varied opportunities to make entry passes.

- With this set, teams can run the screen and roll as well as many other two- and three-man plays.

- The floor can be opened up for one-on-one penetration.

- It adapts to any offensive out-of-bounds situation.

- It incorporates options for each position and each player.

■ You have the ability to continually run options or plays for your better players while giving the defense other offensive looks.

■ It's flexible and creative, and easy to teach, explain and demonstrate.

■ Coaches on all levels will have numerous quick-hitting play opportunities, but the offense will also encourage them to include four- or five-pass continuity that creates movement and forces the defense to constantly adjust to changing offensive tactics.

■ Teams can enter and run plays on either side of the court making them more difficult to scout as well as defend against.

■ Increased scoring chances enable coaches to also emphasize the importance of high-percentage free-throw shooting. When players have more opportunities to score and get to the free-throw line, interest and aggressiveness also increase.

■ The offense encourages three-point plays. Every coach knows that the team attempting and making the most free throws usually wins the game.

Coach's Edge

The box offense puts high-post defenders in the uncomfortable position of defending the high-post pass on a more regular basis, moving them away from the defensive backboard which limits their productivity. Most offenses begin with dribble penetration or screens, a wing pass or flash post setting up a backdoor play from the weak side. Big men aren't used to defending the initial pass in the offense and being away from the basket cuts shot-blocking opportunities.

Coach's Edge

Outstanding defensive transition teams are instructed to never permit a layup or three-point play. On offense, aggressively going the length of the court to the basket forces opponents to defend the entire court. This also disrupts their offensive concentration because they worry about your desire to fast-break at every opportunity. Your relentless penetration may put them in foul trouble and send your players to the free-throw line.

Questions to Consider when Selecting an Offense

1) Can we enter and run plays on either side of the court?

2) Do we have plays or options for each player and position?

3) Do we have a basic set for balance and organization?

4) Are opportunities for transition readily available?

5) Can we run out-of-bounds plays from all areas of the court with this same offensive alignment?

6) Do players have the ability to change positions on the floor?

7) Do we have easily understood keys and symbols or passes to initiate plays?

8) Is this offense effective against all types of full- and half-court man-to-man or zone defenses?

9) Can players comfortably receive the ball in good shooting areas on the court?

10) Can you utilize your players' strengths and minimize their weaknesses with this offense?

11) Does the offense have passing, screening and ball movement opportunities built in?

12) Does the offense have opportunities for continuity as well as one- and two-man pass and scoring plays?

13) Does the offense have the capability to counter and adjust to different defenses, and does it include options for each play?

14) Does it have special play possibilities for different situations?

15) Does it provide good offensive rebounding angles?

16) Will it give you good balance defensively?

17) Do you have weakside movement to occupy the defense?

18) When a player has the ball, is he able to theoretically pass to any of his teammates?

19) Does this offense force defensive players to defend in different or uncomfortable areas of the court?

20) Is the defense forced to make switching decisions and defend mismatches?

21) Does it create one-on-one opportunities to break down the opponent's defense and expose weaknesses?

22) Does this offense provide ample opportunity to penetrate?

Coach's Edge

The box or double high post offense is a tremendous equalizer against defensive pressure or containment because it provides an extra high post press breaker who can get into the middle and attack pressure by being able to receive the ball and then turn 360 degrees and pass.

Coach's Edge

You have a definite advantage on offense if your players are able to play all or most positions because less time is needed to set up the offense in the offensive part of the court. You can enter and begin your offense quickly, giving the defense little time to set up. It never gets a chance to relax. The Chicago Bulls have used this method most effectively in their triple post offense.

Simplified Rules of Offense

- Know your players' habits, strengths and weaknesses.
- Excellent offense depends on passing and movement.
- Always see the ball on offense, not only on defense.
- Watch the man who passes the ball to see what he does to know what your team is doing.
- Cut late rather than early when using a screen without the ball.
- Build the offense by using two-, three-, four- and five-man movements on the half and full court.
- Emphasize spacing, timing, movement, passing, cutting and staggering, and widening your screens.
- Explain why the staggered double is important to proper execution of the box offense.
- Emphasize the importance of penetration, and the penetrate and pitch principle.
- Players must understand and be well-versed in offensive misdirection.
- Each player is responsible for reading the defense.

■ Impress upon players the importance of changing ends in transition and getting behind the defense.

■ Repeatedly stress the importance of taking high-percentage shots. Encourage opportunity shots, but players need to understand that a forced shot is not always the best solution. At times, haste does make waste.

■ Look to create mismatches when the defense is intent on switching men crossing with and without the ball.

Coach's Edge
A player can best free himself by closing the distance between him and his defender, then breaking quickly to the ball. Call this the "cat-and-mouse" principle.

Checklist of Things to Include in the Offense

√ Single and multiple backpicks and screens of all types

√ Circles or loops

√ The pick-and-roll

√ Staggered screens

√ Flex cuts

√ Flaring

√ Triangle screening

√ Misdirection

√ V-cuts

√ L-cuts

√ The "cat-and-mouse" principle

√ Closing the distance

√ Big-man screen across

√ High-low passing and cutting

√ Skip passes

√ Screening for shooters with and without the ball

√ How to screen and free yourself for a shot

√ Clearouts

√ High lob pass

√ Moving with a purpose without the ball

√ Diagonal screens

√ Backdoor or overplay movement and cuts

√ Mismatches

√ Posting up

√ The pinch post

√ Scissoring off of the post

√ Understanding how to read the defense

You must have the ability to penetrate and break down the defense.

Coach's Edge

In our offensive structure, the strong side is always the side of the court with the basketball and the weak side is the side opposite the basketball.

2
Personnel Development

Individual Player Characteristics

In the box offense, players and positions are interchangeable, but the **point guard** is probably the most important because he is most responsible for its direction and execution.

List and discuss the necessary attributes for each position on the floor with your players, then work with them as individuals and in small groups on a daily basis to develop and improve their skills during practice. Establish a routine of a set number of minutes and/or repetitions of each skill during your big and small man drills. Strictly adhere to this method and the principle that "perfect practice makes perfect."

Each offensive player should be able to do these things:

■ Move effectively without the basketball.

■ Understand and know how to get himself free.

■ Be able to establish the triple threat position after receiving the basketball in order to break down the defense and penetrate to the goal.

■ Execute all types of passes — bounce, chest, baseball, underhand, two-hand overhead, etc.

■ Be able to respond to defensive pressure and traps; know how to cut off of and how to utilize screens.

■ To shoot standing still and off the dribble and be able to pass off of the dribble.

■ Be a capable free-throw shooter. High free-throw percentages translate into victories. The team that attempts and makes the most free throws usually wins.

Coach's Edge

Players receiving the ball should know how to get free and establish passing lanes when they want the ball. The "banana cut" or move is a very effective means to get free. To free themselves for a long pass we teach our players to fake and take a step or two to the ball, then reverse direction and go long using the banana cut to free themselves to receive the pass. Reverse the procedure to get free in the other direction.

Point Guard

All skills can and must be continually refined and improved through constant drilling and repetitive perfect practice throughout the season.

- Must be capable of using the dribble to advance the ball, penetrate and either pass or shoot.

- Should be able to shoot off the dribble or from a standing position. Three-point range is extremely important.

- Must be able to read and recognize defenses to help in making correct decisions when calling plays and initiating the offense. He is the coach on the floor and must enjoy making decisions. He must handle the blitz or trap, then punish the pressure defense.

- He is the quarterback who recognizes and adjusts to pressure, double teams and traps.

- Be positively assertive and a team leader.

- Be adept at executing the screen-and-roll.

Coach's Edge

One important point to reiterate: Each player should be confident and a high-percentage free-throw shooter. Work on this every day in practice.

Drills for the Point Guard

1. Dribble entry to the wing area, pass to the low post, cut and return to upblock the high post. Step out after setting the block.

3. Point pass to the high post and screen the ball and then cut away and through.

2. Entry pass to the high post and then the point sets a diagonal downscreen for the player on the weakside low block.

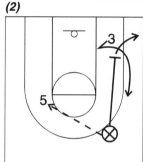

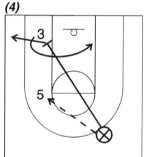

4. Entry pass to the high post and diagonal downscreen for the ballside low post player to set up the curl. Step to corner to open up the court following the curl.

Characteristics of an Outstanding Point Guard

1) He has the ability and desire to make his teammates better players.

2) He's intelligent, has leadership ability, makes good decisions and possesses basketball street smarts.

3) Thinks first about what is best for the team's success.

4) Acts as a coach on the floor during practices. During games he is the coach on the floor.

5) He makes good decisions and is aware of which player is the best choice for a given situation when calling plays.

6) He is responsible for calling the team's plays on the floor.

7) A good defender who doesn't permit penetration by the other team.

8) He displays quickness on the court.

9) Limits his turnovers and strives for a minimum of three assists for each turnover.

10) Has good shot selection, shoots a high percentage from three-point field-goal range and is an outstanding free-throw shooter.

11) Boxes out on defense first, then goes to the best spot to receive the long outlet pass or the second pass to best initiate the fast break. He must constantly work to free himself when overplayed, doubled or denied.

12) Maintains his concentration throughout the game and is a consistent player.

13) He controls the ball, establishes the team's tempo and penetrates with the ball.

Shooting or Big Guard

In a perfect world the **shooting** or **big guard** would have many point-guard and small-forward skills, but first and foremost, he must be a shooter.

- He must cut, catch, dribble and shoot.
- Needs three-point range and accuracy on his shot.
- Have timing and ability to shoot off of screens.
- Must know how to set a screen and then step and recover to get his shot.
- Must know how to move rapidly from a standing position to receive, set up and shoot from any area of the court.
- Know when and how to spot up in shooting areas.
- Should know how to gain position, post up and score.
- Must bring the ball up court and initiate the offense when the point guard is pressured.
- Must use the dribble to execute the screen-and-roll.
- Should have the desire and abilities to rebound.
- Must get out and fill the lane on the transition from defense to offense.
- Have the ability to drive, penetrate and pass, or shoot off of the dribble.

Small or Quick Forward

The **small** or **quick forward** should have many of the same attributes and skills of the shooting guard. If not a pure shooter, he has to score. Normally, he's your best athlete.

- Versatile player and scorer from wings, elbows, perimeter and baseline, and be able to post up and score as well as turn and face his defenders inside.
- Ability and desire to rebound inside and outside.
- Knowledge of how to set and use screens.
- Ability to dribble once or twice and explode to the goal by beating his man off the dribble, then finishing the play in traffic and/or penetrating and pitching to the open man.

■ Must have the ability to advance the ball up court and possibly initiate the offense, relieving pressure on the guards.

■ Have passing skill and the ability to execute both ends of the pick-and-roll. These are both very important skills that the small forward must master.

Coach's Edge

A team's ability to control the offensive re-bound translates into easy and winning baskets. These become especially important at the end of the game during a free-throw or field-goal attempt. The coach must develop this rebound-ing desire and aggressiveness by constantly drilling and stressing its importance during prac-tice.

Center and Power Forward

Ideally, a **power forward** should possess some skills of the small forward and **center**. The center with power forward abilities puts added pressure on the defense.

■ Both should be competent high- and low-post passers.

■ They should be able to hit the 15-foot jump shot, and be capable of faking and then driving to the basket with one dribble from the high post.

■ Ability and know-how to set screens and execute big-man moves from pick-and-roll screens. Many power forwards have ball handling and screen-and-roll skills. An ability to step back and shoot is a major asset.

■ They must be able to feed the post and execute the high post pass.

■ They should know how to pivot and pass when being trapped and how to move from a trap after passing the ball. Stretching the trap using the dribble is important and easily taught.

■ Both must know how to drop step, turn and face, take advantage of the mismatch, know how to pivot to the ball after the screen across, execute the half turn jump shot, execute a baby or jump hook (preferably with either hand), and be able to establish excellent inside post position.

■ Both players should be strong rebounders who like to mix it up, score in traffic and, when fouled in the act of shooting, finish the play and make the free throws.

■ Big men must be able change ends rapidly in transition. The first big man down the floor should get behind the defense as quickly as possible or post up and seal his man. He can accomplish this by running in a direct line from the defensive or rebounding position to his offensive goal. This is the quickest way to move between two points. It not only makes the defense cover the whole court, but also results in easy baskets which we can multiply by immediately pressuring the opponents defensively before they have an opportunity to recover.

Developing the Inside Game

Step-by-Step Individual Moves

1. Turn and face the basket after receiving the ball.

2. Protect the ball with two hands and your body.

3. Locate your defender.

4. Minimize dribbling. Use one, two or none.

5. Make the defense react to you.

6. Hook shot, baby hook and jump hook — high arc.

7. Face up, ball fake, and step up and under.

8. Drop step.

9. Front pivot and drive, and front pivot, cross over and drive.

10. Reverse pivot, and reverse pivot and cross over and drive. When you face and pivot you are able to make four moves on your man by faking one way, left or right, and crossing over and going the opposite way.

11. Screen opposite and turn back to the ball.

12. When using the screen, be quick, but don't hurry; be late rather than early; don't bring the ball down; protect the ball and fake.

13. Fake, drop step and hook.

14. Baseline drive and sitdown move — ball fake — reverse layup and hesitation, feet parallel with end line.

15. Turn and face in low post; full- and half-turn jump shot using both the backboard and then only the rim.

Use of the Arms and Body

- Wide stance

- Present a target.

- Hand or arm over-and-under.

- Advantage of sitdown move.

- How to screen: Screen and seal; screen-and-roll; screen and step back; screen and go immediately; screen and flare; screen from the side, below and top.

■ Screening for the man without the ball: Downscreen; backpick or upblock; side screen for flare, etc; diagonal screen with its options.

■ High and low post: Passing, driving, using the rim to cross under and come back.

Coach's Edge

Placing high post receivers at or above the elbow areas puts extreme pressure on the defense. The elbows are high-percentage scoring areas and great spots from which to pass to the low post, reverse the ball or drive to the basket.

■ How to handle the double team or trap: Pivot, pass, follow and/or stretch; outlet passing after recovering a rebound.

■ How to execute the two-man game from different areas on the floor: Side screen — knees bent on all screens; front screen — arms into chest on all screens; backscreen — right-angle screen; screen-and-roll; screen and stretch, flare or step back; screen and screen again in double reversal; screen and screen away; screen and split the defenders; fake screen and go; screen your defender.

■ Passing: Baseball; two-hand over-the-head outlet; two-hand chest and bounce; high/low pass; pivoting and footwork (possibly most difficult and important task).

Drills

1. Four- or six- and two. One dribble only facing the basket and covering distance. The player must make the basket or rebound his ball before it hits the floor and then finish the play without another dribble.

2. Single, double and hesitation — six different fakes — may only use one dribble to get to the basket from behind the three-point line. We use five different areas of the court for this drill.

3. Mikan drill

4. Sitdown drill

5. Front pivot, and front pivot and crossover

6. One-on-one with your back to the basket — seven attempts (first without and then with a defense).

7. Penetrate to the basket with one and then two dribbles from behind the three-point line. Here we systematically use the direct and crossover dribbles

to the basket, covering distance, but varying our offensive moves. We also drive, stop, fake and shoot the jump shot in this drill which we learned observing the individual offensive practices of the Yugoslavian basketball teams. They normally practice two and/or three times a day and one practice is devoted almost exclusively to individual offensive fundamentals.

8. Milwaukee screening drill with two balls. Two lines screening, curling, and stepping to the ball and shooting from different areas on the court. We use two simultaneous passers in this drill, preferably players.

9. Reverse pivot, and reverse pivot and crossover

10. Finding and locating the defense before an offensive move.

Coach's Edge

It's a good idea to sometimes screen your own defensive man when attempting to set a pick for a teammate. This accomplishes two things: it eliminates the switch by the defense and forces your teammate's defender to go around two men rather than one when chasing his opponent or trying to body-up to him.

Important Ideas to Remember

Never forget the following points:

■ Don't permit opponents to penetrate offensively but create penetrating opportunities for your team.

■ Limit turnovers and offensive fouls.

■ Move without the ball, always changing speed and direction.

■ Pass the ball up court and cover distance without dribbling. If possible, get behind the defense!

■ Try to grab every offensive rebound by anticipating the miss.

■ Always box out on defense and limit second shots by the other team.

■ Rotate back on defense from the weakside.

■ Constantly pass, cut and move without the ball.

■ Against zones and all defenses, always go inside, outside and over, changing sides with the basketball.

■ Learn all team plays, keys and signals.

■ Establish passing lanes and triangles versus zones.

- Use the two-hand over-the-head pass and ball fakes against zones.

- Use normal out-of-bounds plays and their options against all defenses.

- It's better to make a simple play rather than a difficult or spectacular one.

- Don't commit foolish fouls.

- Don't permit a three-point play opportunity on a personal foul.

- Grab loose balls and rebounds with two hands.

- Work to improve and always aim for a high free-throw percentage.

- On defense, use your hands to actively try to deflect passes and limit the opponents' passing lanes.

Coach's Edge

When being fronted or denied, or when receiving contact in the low post, brace and then quickly step to the ball breaking the contact. This may cause the defender to lose his balance enabling you to free yourself to receive the ball and break down the defense.

- Contest every shot your opponents take without fouling them.

- When using screens, cut late instead of early.

- When receiving a pass, always try to establish a good passing lane and target for the passer.

- When trapping the ball, go hard and aggressively; don't hesitate once you have committed yourself.

- Constantly remind players to force the fast break, but not the shot. Make and take high percentage shots.

- When receiving the ball, get in the triple threat position ready to attack.

Coach's Edge

Get the ball to your point guard in passing or scoring position by having him screen for a man without the ball. Then have him step back or cut through the defense without the ball. This wears out his defender and occupies the other defensive players also limiting their help or support capabilities.

Coach's Edge

Teams making the defensive transition and using pressing defenses normally try to pressure the rebounder to prevent a quick outlet pass, stop the outlet from dribbling the ball and deny the closest outlets the ball. Many times this tactic frees the offensive player farthest from the ball. The player who gets in back and into the seams of the defense can cause havoc by attacking it from behind. Effectively executing the long pass in this situation will result in easy baskets and discourage attempts to pressure the ball.

Three special terms to motivate players:

√   Little things win basketball games.

√   Perfect practice makes perfect, rather than practice makes perfect.

√   **K-I-S-S: Keep It Simple Simon**

Coach's Edge
Luck is the residue of design!

Special Situations

Each player must know all plays and options and automatically know what to do in the following instances:

■ Jump balls ... where to tap.

■ Out-of-bounds plays.

■ Two-for-one situations ... quickies.

■ Last shot in period or game.

■ Tie score, down one, two or three points at the end of the game in field-goal or free-throw situations.

■ Offense versus different kinds of zones, man-to-man and pressing defenses on the half- or full-court.

■ How to react in different free-throw situations.

■ Where to slap rebounds and loose balls if you can't control them.

■ How to create a shot or scoring opportunity for a specific player.

■ What to do on mismatches.

■ How to spot up and move to take advantage of trapping by opponents.

■ How to take advantage of an opponent in foul trouble.

■ Signal to let players know there are only five or 10 seconds remaining on the shot clock. They must know what you want them to do in these situations.

Coach's Edge

If properly prepared, players will react confidently under pressure. Compile index cards with special plays for special situations and carry them for reference to use during practice and games.

3
Building a Successful Offense

There are a few questions coaches should ask themselves when designing offensive plays or deciding what type of offense to run. It's advantageous to be able to initiate the same play on either side of the floor and more so if it has two or three entry passing options. The play should provide two or three definite scoring options in order to anticipate and counter any switching, trapping, double-teaming and pressure defenses.

1) Does play selection consider the individual offensive abilities of your players?

2) Are you able to maximize these talents?

3) Who should shoot the ball and from where?

Look for high-percentage scoring opportunities and shot selection. Plays should be designed to penetrate the defense and also make it easy to get the ball to inside people as well as plays that set up open three-point shot opportunities.

A good offensive play provides chances to get fouled. Therefore, proper spacing is a must as is your ability to move and screen effectively without the ball.

Finally, no offensive play is worth its salt unless it provides outstanding offensive rebounding position and backboard coverage as well as proper defensive balance and awareness once the basketball changes hands and the opponent has an opportunity to make the transition from defense to offense.

Objectives of Successful Offensive Plays

- Obtain a good shot for a good shooter in a comfortable area and position on the court.

- Big and small men in triangles, with weakside and defensive balance positions should the shooter miss.

■ Player awareness of each other's strengths and tendencies.

■ Awareness of where most offensive rebounds land or bounce to have a better-than-even chance of getting them and converting them into easy scores.

■ Shooters should be aware that they are the most dangerous offensive rebounders because they know where the miss is going to land.

■ Ability to penetrate the defense.

■ Options should the defense stop your initial move.

Coach's Edge

Most coaches tell their players that the man passing the ball is the most dangerous cutter on the court. He's dangerous because if you read and follow his movement you can easily determine what kind of action will be coming. He'll probably do one of the following:

- Cut to the baseline and stop and then cut to either side
- Bury in the corner
- Inside cut to the ball, then to the near corner or the opposite side of the court
- Screen away or fake and receive a back-screen
- Execute a flare or fade move
- Screen the post or the point of the ball
- Run a pinch post or combine to run a handback with the player to whom he passed the ball

Coach's Edge

In our play execution, we always stress weakside backpicks, screening away, and cutting or interchanging off the ball. This is important when we try to post a player on the strong or ballside block because it occupies the opponent's defense and makes it aware that we constantly look for weakside offensive action. This limits the opponent's concentration on providing weakside help and support defense.

Coach's Edge

Offensive basketball is nothing more than a series of coordinated one-, two- and three-man plays which are executed more successfully if we incorporate weakside movement without the ball into each offensive thrust.

Constructing and Developing a Half-Court Offense

We only have one basketball for 10 players whether the game is 32, 40 or 48 minutes long. Even if each player controlled the ball an equal amount of time he would only have it a total of 3.2, 4.0 or 4.8 minutes. How should players spend the rest of the time on the court? It should be spent helping teammates.

The key to a successful half-court offense is teaching players how to move and work without the ball. This is the coach's responsibility. Without this ability, it's difficult for a team to win consistently.

Coach's Edge

Continually remind your players that basketball is nothing more than one-, two- and three-man plays executed successfully by players helping each other.

Multiple Offenses

In teaching multiple offenses we try to incorporate many things into our basic half-court system. The most important are listed below.

1. In, out and over theory of attack.
2. Timing: When and how to cut without the ball.
3. Use of screens: Cut late, rather than early!
4. How to read the defense. Make it react to you.
5. Playing cat-and-mouse.
6. Moving without the ball.
7. Proper spacing on the offensive end.
8. Changing speed and direction.
9. Using keys and signals.

10. Establishing passing lanes. Who is responsible?

11. The ability to penetrate is the key!

12. Force the fast break and get a good shot.

13. Types of screens: single, double, triple, staggered, shoulder-to-shoulder, downscreens, upblocks, backscreens (screening from behind the defender for misdirection purposes), diagonal (Atlanta and Utah), step-in, and cross-screening.

Leave no stone unturned in offensive preparation!

Coach's Edge

Picking your own defender on offense eliminates the defense's ability to switch when trying to anticipate the play because the switching player is sealed by the man he is defending and is unable to leave him and switch or even help.

The two-man game or pick-and-roll is probably one of the most popular and dangerous weapons in basketball. It might be taught and executed differently in the USA, Yugoslavia or Russia, but the theory is the same: face front or back, know when to release, roll, split, screen away or step back.

We strongly believe in the concept of screening away and often send one, two or three men to set blocks on defenders. As often as possible they should be perpendicular to the defensive man with their knees bent to help them pivot more easily.

Following are breakdown drills we have developed to teach each of the following maneuvers:

1. Screen-and-roll.

2. Screening away.

3. Moving back door or pulling the string when overplayed.

4. The handback and the inside handoff.

5. Give-and-go features.

6. Penetration and pitching, or drawing and kicking.

7. Cutting — strong or weakside without the ball, inside cuts, stepbacks, L cuts, V cuts, various flex moves and shuffle cuts.

8. Catching and setting up your man for the high lob.

9. Post ups or mismatches.

10. Curling or looping.

11. Sealing the defender in the post or to receive on the wing.

12. Crossing — including motion offense movement, corner cuts, diagonal screening techniques, UCLA cuts, and the comeback or buttonhook move.

13. Scissoring or splitting the post.

14. Pivot screens across.

15. Zipper screens — up, down or over.

16. Movement away from the ball.

17. Clearouts and isolations.

18. Last shot or special play deception and closing the distance.

19. Flare move.

20. Dribble weave.

21. Brush block.

Coach's Edge

Spending time teaching multiple offense techniques also improves your defensive preparation since your team has an opportunity to learn how to defend many different types of offensive maneuvers. Remember, a multiple offense includes various elements of today's motion or passing game offense.

One of the most effective teaching methods is to first talk to your players about the offense they will be using, then provide explanations and an overview of what you want to teach. Help your players visualize your explanation by walking through each move without the defense and breaking the offense down into two-, three-, four- and five-man situations and plays. When the players are familiar with what you are trying to teach, put them up against a defense.

At this point you begin to practice with constant repetition, emphasizing execution. In the beginning, stop and correct each error against the various defensive schemes. Forcing your players to execute against different and constantly changing situations helps develop instinctive, automatic reactions and improves players' ability to respond to specific game situations.

We practice against traps, double-teams, pressure and various defensive rotations. Our No. 1 objective is to try to anticipate our opponent's tactics so we may work against them in practice, and learn to react instinctively to any situation confronting us. Continually emphasize how important it is for players to understand why they must be able to penetrate and break down the opponent's defense in order to win. We have developed various transition drills to teach offensive philosophy from the dribble, long pass, rebound, steal or turnover, etc.

In offensive drilling on stack situations, break down every conceivable defensive tactic you might face so that your players have immediate recognition and react spontaneously. This is a continuing process that must be practiced all season because today's innovative coaches are constantly devising new and better methods to defend various situations. Prepare your players to automatically respond to these new developments.

Coach's Edge

Develop special plays for your players to take advantage of each individual's special talents or abilities. This helps them grow and gain confidence as productive and contributing players.

Types of Entry — Initiating the Offense

1. After passing to either high-post player, the entry passer may bury, cut and screen away, screen the point of the ball, handback, fake a cut and replace himself, pinch the post, flare, cut to set up the skip pass, step out, receive a backpick, cut and backpick, dribble and/or receive a staggered or double screen.

2. A penetrating dribble off the high post for the screen-and-roll.

3. Penetrating dribble along the sideline without a screen.

4. Pass to the wing on the sideline.

5. Execute a zipper entry pass after the penetrating dribble.

6. Pass to a flashing post for the backdoor or banana cut option, or drive at the back of an overplaying defender to enable the offensive player to pull the string against his defensive man.

7. Use the high lob pass option over the fronting defender.

8. Screen away and execute the buttonhook option by coming back to the ball.

9. Fake the screen and quickly slide to the hoop.

10. Run the give-and-go option.

11. Use the reverse dribble option.

Coach's Edge

An easy way to get free offensively is to set a screen for another player.

Using a Numbering or Signal System

An innovative method to key plays is by the position of players immediately following each transition. For instance, automatically run one option if the small men are in the high post positions, another if the big men are high. The same holds true if one big and one small are high, and so on. **This requires extensive drilling and concentration, but once mastered is very effective in keying the offense.** Alertness of your players is of paramount importance in making this function correctly.

Here are some suggestions for signals your players can use to key plays or game situations.

- Keying by entry pass or type of entry pass
- Keying by the cut of the passer
- Verbal signals: colors, team names, numbers, states, etc.
- Signs and/or hand signals
- Have other players relay or repeat signals to teammates when pressure is intense or crowd noise is extremely loud
- Have a signal to alert players to the amount of time left on the shot or game clock
- Signal for special need plays in certain situations
- Signals for predetermined situations such as jump balls or free throws
- Plays can be keyed by the position of the opponents' scorer or the player shooting the free throw

Coach's Edge

The player who understands how to change speed and direction has less trouble receiving passes from his teammates and makes him a more effective and dangerous offensive player.

4

Using the Box Offense Against Zone Defenses

The box offense can be an effective weapon against zone defenses. Minor adjustments must be made in your original spacing, but after an initial explanation, the offense is easily adaptable and can be used against any zone.

When attacking a zone defense, keep these rules in mind:

1. Gain control of the defensive rebound, get the ball out quickly and fastbreak from baseline to baseline. This makes it difficult for the defense to establish itself. Force the break but not the shot.

2. Attack a zone from behind and from the weakside without the ball whenever possible.

3. Establish offensive triangles and move the ball in, out and over against and through the zone.

4. Players should utilize two-hand overhead passes and ball fakes and learn to communicate by using eye contact when passing against the zone.

5. Each offensive man should set up between or behind two defenders. This forces defenders to make decisions concerning which men they have to cover adding to the overall difficulty of stopping the offense.

6. Back and side screens are effective against zones.

7. Have players cut through the zone without the ball. Replace these cutters to maintain proper defensive balance and to help you move and reverse the ball.

8. Look for opportunities to pass inside first, back outside and then to the other side forcing the defense to move constantly and react to your ball movement.

9. Look for opportunities to penetrate and pass. Force the zone to collapse and flex.

10. Each player should have his feet planted and ready to shoot whenever he receives the ball.

11. Players should always take a step into the zone each time they pass the ball. This puts them in better shooting position.

12. Rebound every shot from the weakside and from afar. Reminder: longer shots create longer rebounds!

13. Always have the receiver establish a passing lane to make the passer's job easier.

14. The passer should create passing lanes for the receiver by his movement with the ball.

Coach's Edge

When drilling players against zone defenses, make them show the patience necessary to move the defense. To get this point across more effectively in practice, force them to make five passes against the zone before attempting a shot and pass inside once in every three passes. This emphasizes how important the inside game is to successful and winning offense.

Coach's Edge

A good basketball player recognizes situations and who to pass to. The great player creates situations and knows which man is in the best position to receive the ball.

Developing a Zone Offense

Try to develop one offense to use against all types of zone defenses, if possible. It should be an offense which best suits the personnel on your team and utilizes your players in their most productive and efficient areas on the court. Highlight and take advantage of each player's individual strengths.

Your offense should split the defenders to develop clear offensive passing lanes and force the defense to make decisions. Establishing triangles is an effective method to use when attacking a zone defense.

Set screens (side, front and back) for your cutters, shooters and dribblers. Sending cutters, usually your shooters, into and through the zone and reversing the ball to them is a tremendous attack weapon. Send the cutters through after they pass the ball or while someone else has the ball. They can cut from various areas on the floor — baseline, wings, low post or top of the zone — and toward or away from the ball.

Get the ball to your post or pivot men inside the zone. Once they get the ball, they should turn and face the defense and the basket putting them in position to shoot, pass over or through the zone, swing the ball to the other side, or execute a fake to move the defense. If your team is going to be successful, the big men must be offensive threats.

Following are some principles on attacking a zone defense:

1. Always attempt to beat the zone downcourt before it can establish position. Cover the entire court, baseline to baseline, on each possession (rebound, outlet, fastbreak). Force the break but don't force the shot.

2. The objective is always to have a numbers advantage over the opponent. (2-on-1, 3-on-1, etc.)

3. Always pass the ball in, out and over when attacking the zone. Force the defense to continually shift to cover the entire offensive area by changing sides with the ball.

4. Place some players behind it to create and establish passing lanes through the seams of the zone. Try to post up from the baseline where the zone is most vulnerable.

5. Go inside first to make the zone shift and collapse.

6. Try to use two-hand over-the-head passes, ball fakes, bounce passes and penetrating dribbles to dissect the zone.

7. Step into the zone each time you make a pass to get in a better shooting position. Always look for the high-percentage or opportunity shot.

8. Always be in position to shoot. Have your feet, hands and shoulders in the triple threat position when you receive the ball.

9. Dribble penetration is very effective in attacking zones.

10. Rebounders should be in position on both the strong and weak sides anticipating a teammate's shot and ready to crash the backboard to rebound missed shots.

11. Utilize the skip pass when setting screens against the zone.

Coach's Edge

Shooters never worry about getting the ball because they know the ball will always find them if they move effectively to free themselves.

---

12. Always overload the zone; cut through and behind it.

13. Make it a point to show confidence and patience when playing against a zone. Four or five good, crisp passes will make the defense shift and force it to make constant adjustments and decisions.

14. Always try to reverse the ball by passing inside, out and over, forcing the defense to shift and react constantly.

15. Each player must understand what is expected of him or each position and how he is expected to play in the different spots on the court.

Coach's Edge
Always explain, demonstrate and practice. The key is constant repetition and perfect practice.

Checklist for Attacking Zone Defenses

√ As soon as you control the rebound, get the ball out for a fast break as quickly as possible. Push the ball upcourt and search for a good shot before the defense can establish itself.

√ Have your players attack the zone by cutting from behind it and from the weakside into the zone when they don't have the ball.

√ Establish triangles with passing lanes to split and move the defense.

√ Move the ball with two-hand over-the-head passes and ball fakes. The bounce pass can be used in some situations, but ball fakes are extremely important and effective weapons against zones.

√ Communicate by making eye contact with your teammates.

√ Each offensive man should set up between or behind every two defenders forcing both to continually make decisions on whom to cover.

√ Send cutters through the zone without the ball; replace the cutters with the next available offensive man.

√ Pass inside, outside and over (reverse the ball) to move the defense.

√ Using four or five passes and requiring your players to get the ball inside once in every three passes are very effective zone busting techniques.

√ Utilize all types of screens for players with and without the ball as a means of freeing your shooters for good shots.

√ A penetrating dribble to collapse the defense and a pass or pitch outside are very effective in attacking the zone.

√ Each player should have his feet set and be ready to shoot whenever he receives the ball.

√ After making a pass, the player should take a step into the zone creating a better opportunity to obtain a higher percentage shot the next time he receives the ball.

√ Be in position to rebound offensively against the zone by setting up triangles and establishing good weakside rebounding position. Seventy-five percent of missed field-goal attempts come off the side opposite the attempt. Alert players will anticipate missed shots and be in position whenever a shot goes up to grab one or two extra rebounds every game.

√ I feel very strongly that the player receiving the pass is responsible for establishing a passing lane for the player delivering the ball to him. The receiver can best determine if the passer needs assistance.

Zone Sets for the Box Offense

Below and on the following pages are sets to effectively attack zone defenses, create high-percentage scoring opportunities, establish offensive rebounding capability and maintain proper defensive floor balance.

Sending a weakside cutter through the zone from weak side to ball side

1. 1 and 2 throw three passes back and forth which can key 5 to step to strongside corner and 3 to cut to ballside corner. Stepping out gives 5 a better opportunity to screen a baseline defender to free 3 for a shot and an opportunity to pivot to ball and post up after screen.

(1)

(3)
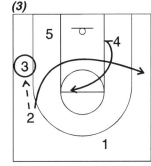

3. 2 passes to 3 and executes the strong to weakside cut. Every cutter should vary the speed of his cut and hesitate and change direction to cause indecision by the defense.

2. 2 can pass to 3 or 5 posting up; he can dribble out from the wing to open the court and spread the defense giving 4 an opportunity to flash into the post and providing another outlet for 2. Once he passes, 2 can cut from to the weak side. Reverse ball through post man or around perimeter to look for high-percentage shots and passes inside.

(2)
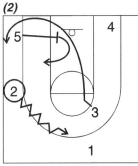

(4)
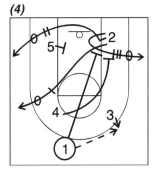

4. Special entry from a high-post pass giving the shooter a scoring opportunity after making one of three possible cuts and after a double down-screen set by the 1 and 4 men. 2 may also come around 3 for a handoff as another option. This play is guaranteed effective vs. zones or man-to-man defenses. The dribble handoff is, as well.

Zone Sets for the Box Offense
1-2-2 Sets

1. *1 makes an entry pass to the wing and weakside low post player breaks to the elbow area from behind the defense. 5 is on the baseline behind the zone's backline defenders, midway between the free-throw lane and the three-point shot line.*

(1)

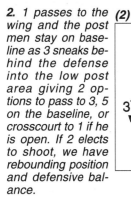

(3)

3. *Entry pass to the wing and 3 cuts through or behind defense to strongside corner. 4 flashes to high post in the middle of the zone. If he receives the ball, he has a 360-degree circle in which to pass to a teammate.*

2. *1 passes to the wing and the post men stay on baseline as 3 sneaks behind the defense into the low post area giving 2 options to pass to 3, 5 on the baseline, or crosscourt to 1 if he is open. If 2 elects to shoot, we have rebounding position and defensive balance.*

(2)

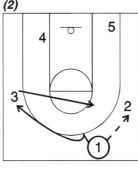

(4)

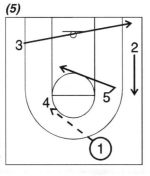

4. *2's options are: pass to 3 in the corner, 4 on the post, 5 on baseline or 1 coming back from the point. On a pass to any of these players, 2 cuts through the zone to the weak side where he's in position to rebound or shoot. This is our in, out and over theory of attacking a zone.*

Post players on or above the elbows and wings spread out in the corners

5. *1 passes to the weakside high post to enter the offense. On the pass, 5 dives through the lane to the baseline and looks for a pass on his cut. 3 stays in corner or cuts baseline and behind zone to opposite corner. 2 slides up to area of free-throw line extended.*

(5)

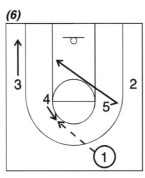

(7)

7. *4 passes to 3 and cuts to the goal area. 2 steps into the zone from behind, 1 establishes a passing lane and 5 posts on the baseline. Any of our players has the liberty to screen for a teammate when we attack zones.*

6. *Same as above but with wings starting out on the wings at the free-throw line extended. On pass to 4, 5 dives, leaving a lane for 2 to step into from the weak side behind the defense. 3 slides and spots up in the strongside corner.*

(6)

(8)

8. *3 has the basketball and we can clearly see his open passing lanes and the triangles we use to attack the zone.*

Zone Sets for the Box Offense

When attacking zone defenses, establish triangles, attack from behind, create open passing lanes, screen, cut, and go inside, out and over. Encourage the use of two-hand ball fakes.

1. Enter using a two-hand over-the-head pass to the wing. Post men cross and cut to the low blocks, watching for a possible pass.

2. The ball is on the wing, the posts are low and the middle or foul-line area is open for a cut by 3 from behind the defense. We prefer to have the shooters attacking the zones from the weak side for the best pass and shot opportunities. 5 and 4 post and 1 spots up on the weak side. 5 always has the option to slide to the corner.

3. 2 has option to pass to shooter (3) at the free-throw line, 5 in the corner or 4 attacking from behind on the low post. On the pass to 5, 4 can post or come to the high post area and/or screen for 3 clearing out to the weak side. 2 can also cut and 1 will replace him to maintain passing lanes, triangles and floor balance.

4. Swing the ball to 3 on the weak side by passing from 5 to 2 and then 2 to 1, or passing through 4 in the middle of the zone where he has a lane to pass to any of his teammates, either inside or outside.

(1)

(2)
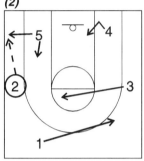

(3)

(4)
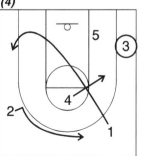

(5)
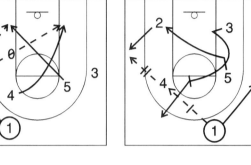

(6)

(7)
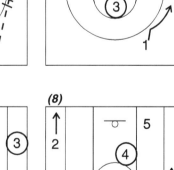

(8)
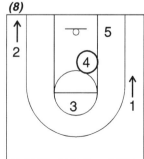

5. Ball is at the point above the zone and 1 must spread the defense by splitting two defenders. He passes to 4 and cuts away, making sure he has provided a passing lane for 4. 4 swings the ball over his head to 2 stepping out from the low block, and 5 dives to the strongside low post providing options for 4 and 2. After 4 passes to 2, 3 comes up to the post, screens 4 and steps out to create a passing lane for 2.

6. 2 has the ball on the wing with passing options to 5 posting or 3 on the foul line. He can skip pass to 1 if he has a passing lane, or 4 who can sneak in behind the defenders from the baseline area.

7. 3 has the ball in the middle of the zone for a shot or pass to any of his teammates. As 4 steps into the zone, 5 may curl behind to establish another passing lane or to occupy the defense from behind and establish weakside rebounding position.

8. 4 has the ball inside the zone and his team has offensive rebounding position, open passing lanes and defensive floor balance.

Zone Sets for the Box Offense

Box set versus man-to-man

1. Once we recognize the zone, both high post players step out to the wings. Post opposite the entry pass breaks high as the other low-post player breaks to the strongside corner behind the defense.

3. This is the setup with the ball in the corner. We have triangles, backboard coverage for offensive rebounds and excellent defensive balance. 5 can post up and turn 360 degrees to pass or shoot once he catches the ball.

2. 3 has the ball on the wing and triangles are set up permitting a pass to 4 in the corner, 1 above the three-point line, and either 5 or 2 in the foul-line area and inside the zone. After his pass, the wing cuts through the lane away from ball. He can hesitate, change speed or the direction of his cut depending on which areas are open. 5 screens for him after vacating post.

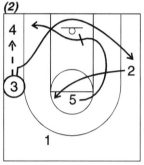

4. From the box we can use the triple post offense by making the entry pass to the wing stepping out and 2 going to the corner as 4 comes to the high post. Or the point man can bury in the corner on his pass to the wing and 2 fill his spot, or by having the 4 man come up to the pinch post. The 2 man can slide to the weakside corner area as well.

Coach's Edge

Remember! When rebounding, the longer the shot, the longer the rebound. Anticipate missed shots no matter which team is shooting.

Coach's Edge

When screening for a teammate, you can avoid confusion, and screen and read the defense better by establishing a rule that the man who wants to set the screen call out the name of the teammate he is screening for. The screen can be set by the player nearest the ball or it can be a backpick set by the player coming from behind the defense from the other side (misdirection).

5

Using the Box Offense with the Fast Break

Fast Break Organization

When running the fast break from the box offense, you must decide whether to teach each player how to handle the responsibilities of each position (point, wing or post) or to limit responsibilities to one, two or all three positions.

I favor teaching players each role, but I also explain how each position should be handled by each individual player. The players must know their limitations and not recklessly undertake tasks they can't execute successfully. The more responsibility you give them, the better they become as players because you are preparing them to handle and react more efficiently and instinctively to pressure and unanticipated situations. The key is exposing them to situations in practices so they can work to correct deficiencies.

Types of Fast Break Possibilities

- Pass or penetrating dribble covering distance
- Sideline break
- Conventional: middle or three-lane fast break
- Cross, turnout, etc.
- Low post
- Trailer or center fielder
- Transition or secondary break
- Early offense and options

Objectives

1. To try and score before the defense can begin to establish itself.

2. To cover the full court area as quickly as possible while looking for the first high-percentage field-goal opportunity. Force the fast break, but not the shot.

3. To distract the opponent's offensive concentration. If you consistently run the fast break, the other team is always aware that you intend to break rapidly once you have the ball. This forces the opposition to make an immediate transition from offense to defense to stop your rapid offensive assault.

4. To constantly outnumber the defense in the initial transition attacks on the goal with 2-on-1, 3-on-1, 3-on-2, etc., scoring opportunities. In these situations, the defense has difficulty helping or double-teaming.

5. To encourage the first big man down the floor to go basket to basket and get behind the defense.

Coach's Edge

A point we repeatedly make and reinforce in practice is that criticism is meant to be constructive and not to be taken personally. We criticize players and their performances to make them better basketball players. This is part of our job and one that must be fully understood and communicated in a positive and healthy environment. It should never be misunderstood nor taken for granted.

Coach's Edge

The coach is not only responsible to prepare his players to win, but also to prepare them to move to and play at the next level of basketball. This is almost an obligatory provision of the player/coach contract.

Deciding When and How to Fastbreak

In 35 years of coaching I have shifted from strict belief in ball control to a strong dedication to multiple offenses and the fast break. We devote a great deal of time preparing to initiate our fast break at every opportunity. Repeatedly scoring easy baskets will demoralize our opponents and keep them off balance. This quick and instantaneous action and reaction also improves the quality and ability of our players since they are exposed to many more situations that occur on the floor and learn to react spontaneously to each of them.

Coach's Edge

If a player grabs every loose ball with two hands and looks upcourt before dribbling, three good things happen — we have the ball, we can see the entire floor and the opportunity to see and hit the open man is not missed.

Always look to fastbreak from the following situations:

1. Steals
2. Interceptions
3. Rebounds on missed field goals
4. After missed and made free throws
5. In-bounds passes following opponents' scores
6. Sideline out-of-bounds possessions in the opponent's backcourt with the referee handling the ball
7. Turnovers
8. Jump balls
9. Saves
10. Deflections
11. Releasing early when the opposition shoots long jump shots
12. From any defensive set, pressure or otherwise, in the back or frontcourt or whenever a transition opportunity presents itself.

Coach's Edge

Quickly covering the length of the court on your fast break or transition spreads the defense and makes it very difficult to stop, contain or succesfully defend your offensive thrust. At this point, the long pass for an easy score is a great tactic. Use it to demoralize your opponent. The Boston Celtics have always used this pass effectively.

Individual Player Responsibilities

Rebounder. Obtain the rebound, pivot and see the court; make the outlet pass or power dribble to advance the ball if outlets are covered.

Receiver. Turn up the floor; try to make an outlet pass to your middle man or primary ballhandler. If he isn't free, push the ball upcourt, covering distance on your dribble until you can pass to an open man, preferably one in front of you. Penetrate!

Wing. Get to the sideline or middle of the court behind the defense as quickly as possible. Be prepared to finish the play.

Low-post player. First big man downcourt. He should run basket to basket (shortest distance to the goal) to score or establish low-post position on the ball side.

Trailer. Get to center field or the high-post position in the middle of the floor to reverse the ball or screen for shooters, ballhandlers or cutters.

Fast Break Fundamentals

- Sideline Break: Your team is able to cover a greater distance faster with a long sideline pass instead of a dribble.

- Low-post players and trailers will get easier shots, easier passing angles and have more room in the elbow area than from the free-throw line.

- It's easier to explain filling the lanes, timing, and when and how to break to the basket.

- Primary Outlets: It's important for the outlets to keep their backs to the sideline because it provides better vision of the entire court, enables the receiver to change the ball from one sideline to the other and virtually eliminates the need to pivot quickly without looking which normally results in offensive fouls.

Coach's Edge

We don't limit ourselves to practicing 3-on-2 or 2-on-1 defensive and offensive transition. We have drills which permit us to work on 3-on-1, 4-on-3 or 2, 5-on-3 or 4 as well as 5-on-5 transition situations. It's very important that the offense recognize and verbalize the defensive alignment confronting it on each fastbreak opportunity. In most cases, the offense wants the ball to stop near the foul line. The defense wants to stop the ball until help arrives and the offense wants the ball near the elbow to exploit the defense in the middle or via a trailer or either wing cutting to the goal for an easy layup.

■ Understanding of and importance of spacing and timing.

■ Different types of outlet passes: Baseball, two-hand over-the-head, two-hand chest, long one-hand bounce.

■ Importance of getting behind and beating your defenders downcourt.

■ High-percentage scoring opportunities in the open court.

■ Ability to penetrate and demoralize the opposition.

■ Releasing early from the opponent's long-range shooters and scoring threats.

■ Multiplying easy baskets by the immediate and aggressive reaction of your team after scoring an easy fast-break basket.

■ The quickest and most efficient way to push the ball up the court is to turn and face before you dribble.

■ Importance of trying to grab all rebounds and loose balls with two hands. Possession of the ball is your primary objective.

Rapid transition is a constant and is consistent with the philosophy of attack. Always try to go full court on each possession. If no fast break or easy basket opportunity presents itself, go full court in, out and over. Cross or flare your wing men and screen from the ball side unless signaling otherwise. Also try to attack the defense from behind which is consistent with our rules for attacking a zone.

It's always the intention to pass to the lead offensive player if he is free. This rewards the player who works hard to get behind the defense on the fast break or transition and continually places pressure on the opponents to get back and defend which interferes with their ability to concentrate offensively.

There are a number of breakdown drills to use when teaching fast-break organization. Like most coaches and comedians, some should be revised or refined, but most aren't original. They were taken from other people in the field.

Coach's Edge

Good things will happen if your team can move the ball the length of the floor and inside, out and over. You'll be in position to score inside, pass to cutters or spot-up shooters, rotate and reverse the ball, collapse the defense, and establish and command great offensive rebounding position.

Fast-Break Options After a Missed or Made Free Throw

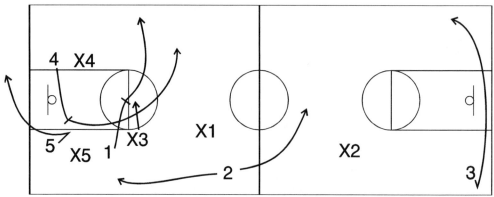

We normally have 4 and 5 in the rebounding spots closest to the basket when our opponents are attempting a free throw. Our point guard plays the shooter. His first responsibility is to box out the shooter and look for the long rebound off a miss, then go across the lane to the opposite side of the court above the foul line extended with his back to the sideline as an outlet in position to receive the first pass after a make or a miss. He can now immediately see the entire court to start our fast break without first having to pivot or turn. The designated inbounds passer after a successful free throw is the rebounder nearest the basket who was lined up on the same side as our point man. We have our other guard or ball handler (2) at midcourt on the same side as our point guard which gives us outlets on either side of the court once the shot has been attempted. The small forward (3) or best three-point shooter is down at our offensive baseline behind the defense, preferably in the corner, where he is in position to shoot the three-pointer. We are now prepared to run our offense the full length of the court and have spread the defense, giving ourselves better and clearer passing lanes and penetrating options.

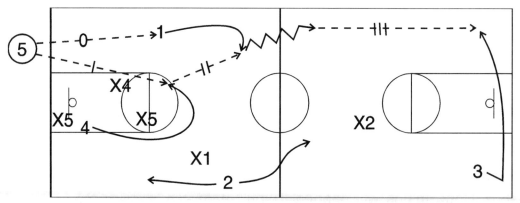

This is our alignment after our opponents have made the free throw and we are inbounding the ball: 5 inbounds from the side opposite his free-throw lane position when he lined up for the shot and after he has boxed out. He is now once again on the same side of the court as 1, our primary outlet. 5 is outside the free-throw lane and away from the backboard because we don't want the backboard to interfere with his ability to throw a long inbounds pass. If the ball hits any part of the backboard on a pass from out of bounds it's a violation and results in a loss of possession. 5's first responsibility is to inbound the ball safely. Each player must realize that the first pass following an opponent's score maintains possession and the second breaks the pressure which enables us to fastbreak and score quickly. Our second option on the inbounds pass, if 1 is covered, is to 4 posting in the middle. 5 may run out of bounds along the baseline to the other side of the basket (he has 5 seconds) to inbound the ball to 2, as well. Once the ball is safely in play, we look upcourt for 1 cutting to the ball or long to 3, who has cut to the ball side behind the defense. Our objective is to cover as much ground as quickly as possible, using long passes or dribbles that cover distance, to score quickly and put tremendous pressure on the defense.

Fast-Break Options After a Missed or Made Free Throw

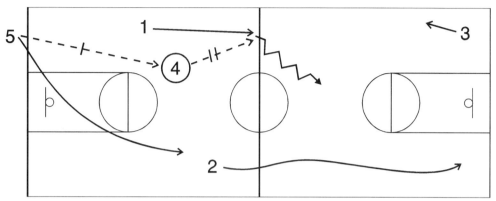

The inbounds pass is made to 4 who immediately turns and looks upcourt for 1, 2 and 3, each of whom is attempting to get free to establish a passing lane to receive the first pass. 5 steps in at a 45-degree angle after making his pass and gets upcourt to provide another outlet for 4 and also to beat his defender downcourt on the transition or fast break. If we inbound to 1 or 2, our cuts remain the same; we try to get to open areas to spread out and exploit the defense. Our goal is to score high-percentage fast-break baskets as quickly as possible. By establishing a numbers advantage, we create more high-percentage scoring opportunities. If we don't have the fast break, we execute our organized transition attack, covering the length of the court with the basketball. We then look to cross the players filling the wing positions, run turnouts, triangles, UCLA screens, curls, backpicks and flex cuts. We want to reverse the ball inside, outside and over whenever possible and we look to employ any of the two-man game options. Our objective is to put as much pressure as possible on the defense, forcing it to stop us before it can get back and organize.

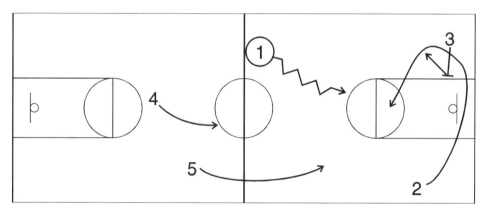

The point guard (1), has the ball with an opportunity to run a sideline fast break, opening up the center of the court for trailers or he can take the ball to the middle, outside the elbow area and look to run the more traditional three-lane fast break. I prepare my teams to run both types because in a game you must take what the defense gives you. I want the players to recognize the defense, how many defenders are back and select the most advantageous and effective plan of attack. We instruct the player with the ball on the break to slow down, change his speed and even the point of attack once he has crossed the midcourt line by changing direction and crossing over with the dribble to the other side of the court. This goes against the grain of the retreating defense and gives the player with the ball a better view of the defense and helps him make a decision that will lead to an easy basket. We use the same basic plan when rebounding a missed or made free throw, and we practice this fastbreak organization each day, both with and without a defense, challenging our players to score in less than three seconds. Practicing things rapidly and imposing time limits aids in skill development and the positive reaction of players when they face pressure.

Fast-Break Options After a Missed or Made Free Throw

(1)

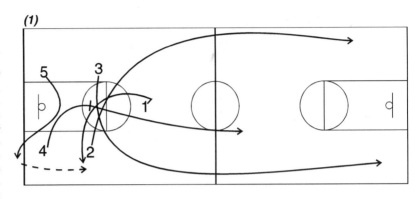

Here are three additional box sets used on free-throw alignments. Each is designed to enter the ball to the point guard. Many teams have the big man who does not grab the rebound or inbound the ball set a screen to free the point guard which enables the point to receive the outlet pass in position to advance the ball upcourt.

Some teams try to score rapidly after a made or missed free throw while others are content to bring the ball upcourt and immediately begin to run their transition offense.

(2)

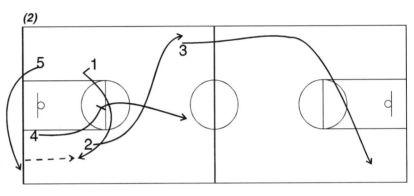

Of course, teams will vary their attack depending on the score or game situation when the free throw is attempted.

(3)

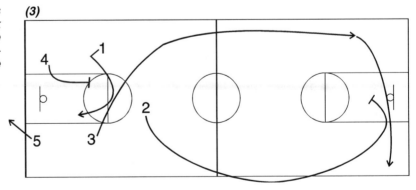

6
Terminology and Options

Types of Moves in the Box Offense

1) Backdoor move

2) Buttonhook

3) Curling

4) Cutting ... L, V, weakside, flex and shuffle

5) Dribble clearout

6) Flare move

7) Give-and-go play

8) Handback action and inside handoff

9) High-low action

10) Isolation ... different players and court areas

11) Lob or alley-oop play

12) Misdirection action and screening

13) Pick-and-roll or two-man game

14) Pinch post action

15) Screening ... across, backpicks with skip passes, downscreens, sidepicks, staggered screens, slash, multiple screens (double and triple), baseline, and diagonal up and down

16) Stacks ... double and triple

17) Triangle action

18) Turnouts

19) UCLA action

20) Weave action

21) Zipper moves

Players must realize that each fake or move included in the offense is there to help the team and permit players to free themselves and increase scoring opportunities. Each move or fake sets up the next and provides more options to run plays by relieving the defensive pressure opponents put on the ball.

We work and drill constantly during the season helping our players develop and improve their skills, not only in dribbling, shooting, screening and passing, but also faking, moving and learning how to free themselves to create better scoring opportunities and remain one step ahead of the defense. This is consistent with our philosophy of developing fundamentally sound, unselfish and versatile players.

Coach's Edge

Players really have no limitations. The only limitations they have occur when coaches tell them they cannot master something. If we challenge them to achieve, they may make mistakes at first, but their desire to succeed will enable them to learn and improve. The coach has an obligation to develop the best player possible and to help each player attain the goals he has set for himself.

Explanations of Each Move

The following are plays that need to be demonstrated. For emphasis, we try to use the name of a prominent player or coach who has made effective use of each play.

Backdoor — also called the Blind Pig. Demonstrates pulling the string on an overplay or denial. We can make use of the lob or bounce pass, or a flash post and banana cut in our execution. (Coach Al Lobalbo)

Backpicks and Sidescreens — screen and step-out or pop-out by the player who has just passed the ball or for another teammate without the ball. The screen may be at a right angle to the defender or directly behind him. It's the cutter's responsibility to set up his man for the backscreen. Great scorers realize that setting a backscreen is the best way to get themselves a great shooting opportunity.

Big Man Screen Across — these screens are executed opposite across the lane, parallel high posts or elbows. They may be horizontal, vertical or diagonal from high to low or low to high. You may have a slash screen opposite, a lob situation or even a screen away from the elbow to the wing, but each screener must read the cutter's movement, turn and face the ball, and cut to an open area, pinning the cutter's defender. This creates two viable options for the passer and takes away the defensive help. Hakeem Olajuwan and Otis Thorpe were experts at this move when they played together for Houston.

Brush Blocks — when a passer goes away in the direction of a teammate and the teammate uses the passer's cut as a screen without actually waiting.

Clearout — sometimes called iso or isolation. The passer can pass to the wing, elbow, high post or other area of the floor and cut away to isolate or free an offensive player for a one-on-one opportunity. You may have different options for different players. (Kareem Abdul-Jabbar or Michael Jordan)

Crossing Action — used in transition or a set offense, this normally occurs on the baseline, but I have seen it used effectively on the high post or elbow area by a number of European teams. You may cross under the basket or outside the paint and move to the corner and fade, cross to the wing area, execute a UCLA upblock, screen up diagonally across the lane for the opposite high post or trailer, cut up the middle to an open area or buttonhook and post up in the lane following the cross (Boston Celtics' Larry Bird). An uneven crossing set-up helps eliminate equals switching and our over-and-under crossing accomplishes the same thing. Cutting between defenders when crossing with the ball leaves one offensive man free and also opens up a side of the court for him in case the defense tries to trap.

Curl or Loop Action — you may curl around the post man or the man setting the screen on any area of the court. Following the curl, the stationary offensive player may post up or step out for a one-on-one opportunity. You may curl off a downscreen and also on a baseline cut move. I have seen this moved used effectively by UCLA, the Portland Trailblazers, and in the unbalanced slash cuts of Utah, Atlanta and Houston of the NBA. Dino Radja had a set play run for him from the low post while playing for Roma in Italy before playing for the Celtics.

Cutting — this is in reality moving without the ball on offense and is one of a team's most important offensive weapons. Your players must master movement utilizing screens but they must watch the ball and their defenders to know when, where and how to cut without the use of a screen. Some cuts that should be taught and used are the V and L cuts, weakside cut to the ball, bury, baseline stop and read, UCLA cut from the top, when to move on the pin down, ball or weakside zipper, splitting the post cuts, shuffle, buttonhook pin and seal, diagonal Utah and Atlanta cuts, and the flex cut from the corner. U.S. Senator Bill Bradley was a master of this while playing for the New York Knickerbockers and Michael Jordan always gets free by moving without the ball at crunch time.

Diagonals — high-low unbalanced up or down screens emphasized by Atlanta and Utah in the NBA using small on big, big on big, and big on small. This is Karl Malone's "money move" for the Utah Jazz.

Freeing Guards from Man-to-Man Pressure — this opens the floor for the guard being pressured by having the guard without the ball split the two backcourt defenders. This was a tactic used by Red Holtzman and his great Knicks teams with Walt Frazier and Earl Monroe in the backcourt.

Flare Cuts — this is a move, normally by a backcourt man immediately after he passes the ball or without the ball when a weakside big man sets a blind high screen on the offensive man's defender. It's used to free shooters being tightly guarded.

49

The man using the screen can go over the top of the screen and slide to the wing or corner, cut inside and bury to the wing for a skip pass, or fake the flare and dive inside, a move used effectively by Paul Westphal when he played for the Phoenix Suns. Dick Snyder also used this move for the Cleveland Cavaliers under Bill Fitch. The screener also may dive to the basket when his defender tries to slow down the player executing the flare.

Give-and-Go — pass, fake (freeze your defender) and cut to the basket for a return pass. (Magic Johnson)

Handback or Pass and Return to the Ball — a very good tactic to use when you want to set up a lob play, screen-and-roll, clearout or simply relieve pressure on the man with the ball. Another of Magic's moves to run his opponent ragged.

High Post Flash — Breaking to the ball from behind the defense to relieve defensive pressure and set up the back door.

Lob Pass Moves — pinning your defender on your back in the lane, fake, and go on the overplay and reverse pivoting when overplayed out on the floor. This is a great play to use when a Shawn Kemp or Dominique Wilkins is being overplayed.

Misdirection — men away from the ball set picks on the baseline crossing action and on the pick-the-picker action. All screens away from the ball are of the back pick variety so the defender must always be looking over his shoulder for a back screen. This would include zipper type upblocks. When Del Harris coached the Milwaukee Bucks he used this tactic especially for Jack Sikma.

Penetrate and Pitch — movement by the man with the ball to draw defenders to him and enable shooters to spot up. B.J. Armstrong and John Paxon of the Bulls used this strategy.

Picking the Point of the Ball — action where a man passes to a teammate and instead of cutting, screening or moving away, immediately follows his pass and attempts to screen the receiver's defender. In today's basketball, many small forwards, power forwards and even a few talented centers can use the dribble in penetrating situations. Coaches should not limit the two-man game dribblers to the guards. This move also sets up the effective but not frequently used inside handoff.

Pin-Down Screen or Upblock Action — these screens can be single, double or triple, staggered or together, and from the strong or weak side. They can be flat or diagonal. Normally, but not always, a big man screens for a smaller man. Bradley used this screen effectively with Willis Reed when they played together for the Knicks with Dave DeBusschere the passer. Today, Reggie Miller earns great money from this play.

Pinch Post Option — this normally occurs when a guard passes the ball to a postman in the elbow or higher post area, then either cuts off of the receiver for a handback, buries in the corner, clears out, or receives the ball back on the wing to run the pick-and-roll. The post-up player is also in a great position to pivot and face the basket, and take his man one-on-one. This is a primary weapon of the Chicago Bulls' triple post offense.

Pick-and-Roll — the two-man game or screen-and-roll is a primary tool of today's NBA and European professional teams. It was also a very effective weapon for Frank McGuire's great teams at North and South Carolina and Joe Mullaney's Providence College teams when Lenny Wilkens played. Chuck Daly coached Detroit to two NBA championships with it.

It can be used effectively by many different players from the corners, elbows, wings, middle and top of the floor. The point guard can reverse the dribble when overplayed and the big man can always reverse pivot and reset the screen. The picker can split the defense, step back for jumpers, hold the screen and cut to the basket for a return pass, or come up and fake setting the screen.

Screening — there are many different types of screens and many may be set more effectively in many different areas of the floor. The different screens are the pin down, backpick, side, downscreen, staggered, down and up again, high post screen across, diagonal screen, and pivot and baseline flex. They can, as previously mentioned, occur on the strong or weak side of the court.

Coach's Edge

Another feature of the box is that plays may be designed to include many different offensive tactics and maneuvers. This flexibility is evident when one looks at the pinch post series which incorporates not only this option but also the screen-and-roll, curl, handback, multiple screens and isolation options.

Scissors or Splitting the Post — still used but not as much as when Dick Motta coached the Chicago Bulls, Jack Ramsey the Portland Trailblazers or Red Auerbach the Boston Celtics. Phil Jackson's Bulls probably use this play more than anyone today. It depends on an exceptional passing big man and is used in Tex Winter's famed triple post offense.

Once the pass is made to a post player, two men usually split or cross over the top of him with the passer normally going first. The two players can cut to the basket, fake the split and cut straight down, screen for one another and go, or step back and cross, cut or screen for other teammates.

Stacks — single and double along the free-throw lane on the baseline or elbow areas. The shooter is normally the bottom or lower man and another shooter usually crosses, curls or runs off of the stack. Daly's Pistons used this for Joe Dumars, Isiah Thomas and Vinnie Johnson. I have also seen and used a single-triple stack with very good results because, like misdirection screens, the triple is not used as frequently and teams are not as well prepared to defend it.

Staggered Screens — at times much more effective than the shoulder-to-shoulder screens. A defender is forced to get through two or three screens instead of one. The screens usually occur along the baseline, in or alongside the free-throw lane and adjacent to the elbow or high post area causing big men to switch out on small men. This creates mismatch opportunities for the offense. Pat Riley's Los Angeles Lakers used this very effectively.

Triangles — normally a continuity move utilizing the pick-the-picker principle with a cross screen and an upblock or down screen. It also utilizes the misdirection screen philosophy which is often hard to defend. It provides shooters with great shot opportunities.

Turnout — I saw this used most frequently in the middle 1970s by the Boston Celtics' John Havlicek when Tom Heinsohn was his coach. The Celtics would cross on the baseline in their transition and fade to the corner, cross to the wing and/or curl. Since then I have seen and we have added diagonal upblocks and UCLA up-blocks for trailers, straight cuts up the middle and various screening techniques to free our men cutting on the baseline to force the defense to make more decisions. We also utilize the screen and post in our turnout series.

UCLA High-Post Cut — the cutter may cut to the baseline and wait for the pin down, he may return and back pick the high-post player, go halfway into the lane and screen the other high-post player in the box series and step out, backscreen the wing, pick the other low-post defender or diagonally screen across to the elbow area and/or clear out to the weak side of the court. A great move for a shooter is to pass to the wing, cut below the high post and backscreen him, and then step out or fake the cut and pop back for a return pass and an open shot. The fine Australian shooter Andrew Gaze used this move successfully when he played for Seton Hall during the Pirates' run to the NCAA championship game in 1989.

Weakside Cuts — Pete Newell, the great California coach, used the weakside crossing cut in his motion offense. He should get credit for motion and also for attacking and spreading the defense by opening the court and cutting through it from the weak and strong sides using timed crossing action. This cut takes advantage of the defender who tries to cheat, double-team, trap or likes to turn his head to watch the ball after it is passed.

Weakside Low Post Duck-In — effective move from the low post. The offensive player seals his defender, steps into the lane and presents a great target when the high post player with the ball is in a position to reverse the ball or pass inside. Great move for Shaquille O'Neal.

Weave — two or more men spreading the defense and dribbling, screening and handing off on an angle. They also look to split the defense by preventing the switch which can result in an easy basket.

Zipper Action — the action most widely used in the box offense. There are many different types of cuts and screens and the teams most successful with this offense have players whose timing and reading of the defense is extremely astute. You can zipper down, up, front, backscreen, angle slash, fade, flare, go over or under, cross, curl, cut or screen diagonally, and clear out. Waiting for the screen and then breaking rapidly to the ball or open area puts a tremendous strain on the defense and makes it extremely vulnerable.

When constructing an offensive play, the defense — any defense — has difficulty defending plays that cause it to switch men of unequal size, especially when a small man screens a big man in the lane or close to the basket. In addition, defenses have trouble defending backscreens and misdirection plays, diagonal screens, big men screening across the lane, staggered screens, multiple screens, clearouts and the two-man game. As a result, we try to include **three** of these tactics or options in each of our offensive plays.

Coach's Edge

Ed Krinsky, a successful Long Island high school coach who developed many college and professional players, devised a unique system for having his team call its plays. The name of any state might designate one play, any color another, an NBA team's name a different play and single- and double-digit numbers for others. I'm sure there are many other creative ways to signal plays that a coach could devise to confuse opponents and scouts.

Diagrams to Demonstrate Each Move

1. Backdoor: *Guard dribbles at the wing man. Wing man takes step to the ball and executes a "V" cut, then makes sharp cut to the goal and looks for return pass.*

(1)

(5)

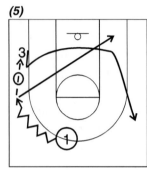

5. Clearout or isolation: *1 dribbles into wing area; 3 fakes toward ball, then clears out across the lane leaving 1 with a one-on-one opportunity. 1 may pass to 3 in same situation and cut across lane giving 3 a one-on-one opportunity.*

2. Backpicks: *Once 5 has the ball in low post, 3 will move up the lane and set a backpick for 4. High post man (4) must wait until 3 is stationary. He then executes a cut behind the pick to the goal. He also has option of cutting inside the screen to the goal.*

(2)

(6)

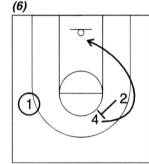

6. Sidescreen: *As 2 is almost parallel to 4, he comes from weak side and sets blind screen on 4's defender. 4 reverse pivots over the top and cuts to the goal. 2 then steps back from goal to provide outlet for man with ball.*

3. Big man screen across: *4 crosses the lane, sets screen for 5. Following the cut by 5, 4 pivots on his left foot and turns back to ball. 5 reads defense and cuts high or low. 4 pivots in opposite direction.*

(3)

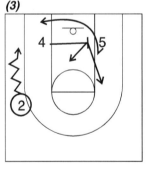

(7)

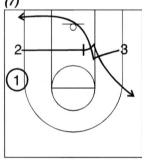

7. Wings crossing on the baseline: *Ballside wing screens across lane to set pick for man crossing from weak side. 3 waits until screener stops and then cuts over or under to the ballside corner.*

4. Brush blocks: *With ball on the wing, 2 cuts away in 3's direction but doesn't screen. 3 waits until 2 passes and immediately cuts off of the back of 2 down the lane to the goal.*

(4)

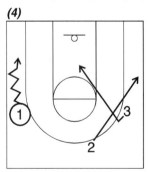

(8)

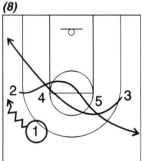

8. Wings crossing on elbows: *1-4 set with wings cutting over and under high post men. Wing on the ball side cuts first; other wing reads his cut and does the opposite.*

Diagrams to Demonstrate Each Move

1. Curl or loop: With ball on wing, 2 cuts across lane, circles under then over 5 and returns to his original position or cuts high, freeing himself for a pass or freeing 5 in low post if his man follows 2. Many NBA teams use the 2 and 3 men to create mismatches on switches.

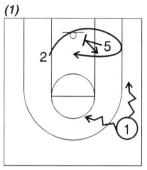

2. Curl or loop option: In zipper set with ball on the wing, 2 cuts down and inside the lane around and over 5. This frees 5 or 2 and also permits 5 to step to corner to receive a pass and open up the court.

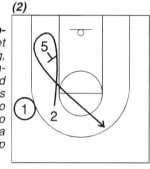

3. Cutting without the ball: With ball on the wing, 3 fakes and executes a diagonal weakside inside cut to the ball.

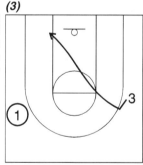

4. Point guard passing, executing inside cut and burying in corner: Provides an excellent passing angle to the low post and sets up a 3-5 screen-and-roll opportunity

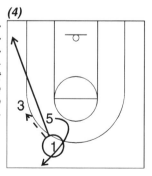

5. Diagonal high to low downscreen with ball on the wing: 3 waits on the low post for a screen from the opposite high post and then cuts up high to receive. This gives the player with the ball two entry pass options.

6. Diagonal low to high backscreen and step out: Again we have diagonal screening by players of different size. This also provides excellent corner passing angles as well as a 1-2 hand-off or screen-and-roll option

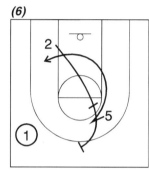

7. Give-and-go cut: point passes to the wing, executes a "V" fake, cuts to goal for return pass. The "V" cut and fake may be executed toward or away from ball.

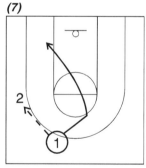

8. Give-and-go: Wing passes to the post, fakes and cuts down lane for the ball. Very effective when wing's defender turns his head to look at ball.

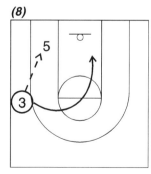

Diagrams to Demonstrate Each Move

1. Freeing the guards from man-to-man pressure: *1 has ball, 2 cuts in front of his defender and behind 1's defender to eliminate the switch and open the court for the ball handler.*

(1)

2. Freeing the guard after horizontal entry pass: *1 passes to 2, cuts in front of his defender and behind 2's defensive man to open the court for man with the ball and also eliminate switch by the defense.*

(2)

3. Flare cut by passer: *Following his pass to one post man, point guard fakes to ball then cuts away using backscreen set by weakside post man. He may physically run his man off the screen or cut over or under screener to wing area. Many teams use this to post a bigger point guard.*

(3)

4. Flare cut for guard without the ball: *Weakside post man sets a backscreen for the man without the ball to free him for a shot. Player receiving screen can cut over or through the lane for a return pass. Depends on the defense being played.*

(4)

(5)

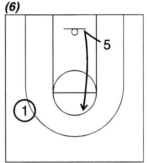

5. Handback: *Point man passes to wing, fakes a "V" cutaway and returns to again receive ball. Before receiving the handback he makes another "V" cut to make it difficult for defender to deny the return pass. If denied the pass, he can cut to hoop as in the give-and-go.*

(6)

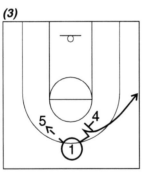

6. High post flash: *Low post fakes into lane then flashes high to receive ball. This sets up the pinch post or backdoor. The flash can come from the strong or weak side.*

(7)

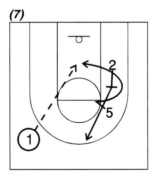

7. Lob pass with low post backpick: *Weakside upblock along free-throw lane to permit high post to fake to ball or freeze his man and then cut behind screen to basket. He may or may not use a reverse pivot to get free.*

(8)

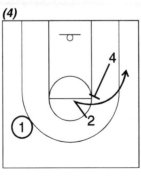

8. High-low pass: *Ball on wing and low post is fronted or played on the side (3-4). Ball handler passes to high post; when low post man seals his defender he receives a pass in the lane from high post.*

Diagrams to Demonstrate Each Move

1. Misdirection backpicks away from the ball: *With ball on the wing, 4 sets vertical backpick for 5 and then 3 sets horizontal screen across the lane for 5. The second screen may create a mismatch if switched.*

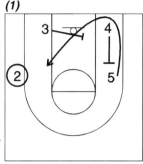

(1)

(5)

5. Screening or picking the point of the ball: *Here the point passes to the wing and goes directly to the ball to set a screen for a two-man game opportunity.*

2. Penetrate-and-pitch: *1 uses high side screen from 5 to penetrate to the middle of the court, drawing 3's defender to help. 3 fades away or circles to the ball creating a passing opportunity for 1 if he can't penetrate.*

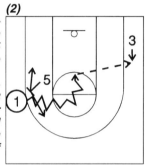

(2)

(6)

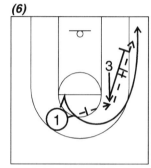

6. Post-to-wing return pass *and pick the point of the ball by the player making the return pass.*

3. Wing-to-middle penetrate-and-pitch: *3 uses a screen by 5 to drive to the middle. If he is stopped, he may pass to a free man in front or back to the free man in the corner on the same side (skip pass option).*

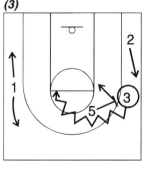

(3)

(7)

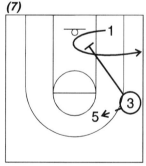

7. Pin down wing-to-baseline pick or screen: *Wing passes to high post and screens down on the baseline. Player on baseline waits for screen, then cuts up or into the lane to receive a pass from high post. Screener turns and looks after the curl by 1.*

4. Penetrate-and-pitch when wing is forced to the corner: *On this option it's important to emphasize the importance of spotting up to get free and help establish clear, viable passing lanes.*

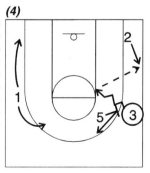

(4)

(8)

8. Upblock from baseline to wing after wing passes to the high post: *After passing, the wing fakes high and waits for a screen from baseline player or a lob pass or post-up situation.*

Diagrams to Demonstrate Each Move

1. Pinch post option: *Pass from point to wing, point fakes down then cuts to ball for return pass as he rubs his man off of the post. Similar to handback move on the wing but used here with a post man as in triple post offense. Cutter can continue to wing if he doesn't receive return pass which provides post with more opportunities.*

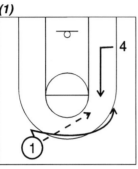

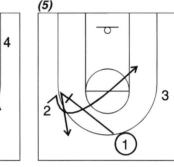

5. Pass to wing, screen away and step back to the ball: *The player receiving the screen must wait for the screen to be set. He may cut over or under. By waiting, he permits the wing to penetrate to the basket, etc.*

2. Screen-and-roll elbow to wing: *With ball on the wing, post man moves horizontally to the ball and sets a screen on the ball handler's defender. He may face the ball or pivot and set the screen with his back to the ball. The latter move is more common at the international level.*

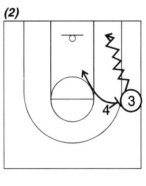

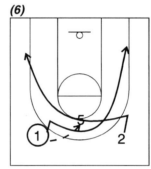

6. High-post scissor or splitting the post: *Normally, player passing to the post cuts first. He cuts over the post and goes directly to the basket, or he stops and sets a screen for the other player also splitting the post.*

3. Screen-and-roll low post to corner: *Same as previous move. In each screen-and-roll situation the screener may roll to the basket or step back to receive a pass.*

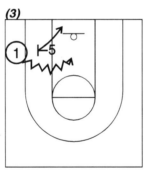

7. Splitting the low post from the corner or the wing: *Same as previous diagram but the pass to the post comes from either player.*

4. Baseline or low post to wing two-man game: *Same principle as two previous diagrams with low post moving high to screen the wing.*

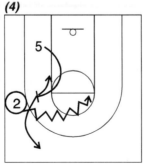

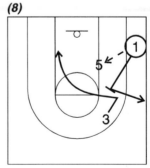

8. Splitting the post with the fake split: *After pass to the post, second cutter fakes the split and cuts backdoor to the basket when be is overplayed.*

Diagrams to Demonstrate Each Move

1. Balanced double stack on the baseline: *On predetermined read of the ball, one of the low men cuts one way and the other moves in another direction. It's the responsibilty of the point man to deliver the ball to the free man whether it's a wing or post man.*

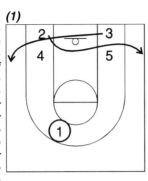

2. High double stack on elbows: *Same as previous diagram but wings may cut over and/or under to free themselves and also screen for the other player.*

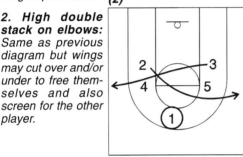

3. Staggered baseline screens: *Two successive screens for the wing in the lane. Wing must not cut too soon and must hesitate to set up and move his defender into both screens to best free himself for a shot or free one of the screeners if the defense switches.*

4. Staggered vertical screens along the free-throw lane: *Again, man receiving the screen must wait until it's set before he moves.*

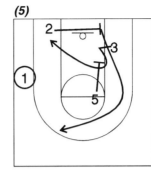

5. Triangle and/or pick-the-picker screen: *Horizontal screen across free-throw lane with the ball on the wing, then a vertical downscreen for the first screener.*

6. Triangle horizontal backscreen: *Low man away from ball sets vertical backscreen across the lane and to the ball, then posts up or steps to the corner. The man receiving the first screen then vertically backpicks the high post and steps out to the ball.*

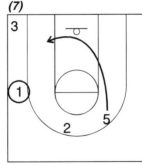

7. *Triangle options for the passer or man with the ball after or while the screens are set.*

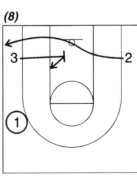

8. Turnout: *Wing on strong side sets screen on the near-side block for the other cutter. Both wings have many options on their cuts. Used effectively in NBA because zones are prohibited. Used by 2 and 3 men, and includes circles and other options to create mismatches and cause defensive indecision on switches.*

Diagrams to Demonstrate Each Move

1. Turnout and circle off the weak side: *Occurs when weakside wing has reached the block on ball side before wing has had time to set a screen. He simply cuts and circles back to the corner, executing a move which is unexpected and difficut to defend.*

(1)

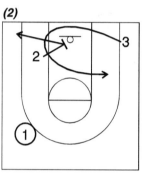

(5)

5. Weakside low post duck-in: *With ball on the strongside high post, the weakside low post man fakes a step up the lane and flashes to the low post to receive a pass in the lane.*

2. Turnout, circle and step back: *Synchronized move on wings crossing after the ballside wing sets the screen.*

** It's important to include all of the various screening techniques and backpicks into the turnout series to make the defense switch, forcing it to make constant decisions and adjustments.

(2)

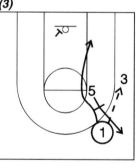

(6)

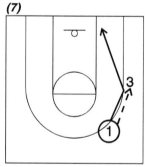

6. Weave: *Dribble and screen action from the wing to the corner to the point. Actually a dribble handoff. It's the responsibilty of man receiving the pass to fake, set up his man and create a penetrating passing angle on the handoff.*

3. UCLA vertical point cut after he passes to the wing: *Point cuts inside to ball or down the lane depending on defense. After post man screens the point, he steps out for the ball. The point may cut, stop and return, or set a backpick for the post man.*

(3)

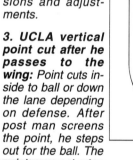

(7)

7. Inside handoff: *Pass from the wing to the point. Point fakes a cut around the wing and executes an inside cut between his defender and the ball and also between wing's defender and ball for a return pass and easy basket.*

4. Weakside diagonal inside cut: *With the pass to the strongside wing the weakside wing, cuts inside his man from the weak to the strong side through the lane.*

(4)

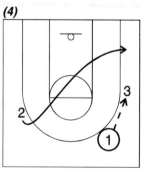

(8)

8. Zipper option: *Strongside vertical inside downscreen, post up and step back.*

Diagrams to Demonstrate Each Move
Zipper Moves

1. Strongside pindown and outside cut: *It's important, as always, that the baseline man wait until vertical downscreen is set before he cuts to free himself. Correct timing will free both players more effectively.*

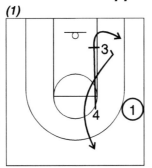

(1)

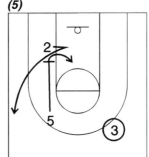

(5)

5. Weakside vertical downscreen: *Pop out and post up.*

2. Vertical downscreen and circle to corner: *Low post player waits for vertical downscreen, fakes in or up and circles to the corner.*

(2)

(6)

6. Weakside vertical downscreen: *Circle and pop out for an isolation.*

3. Vertical downscreen and circle: *Baseline man again waits for screen, then curls over the screener once screen has been set. He may also circle under the screener and step to the strongside corner.*

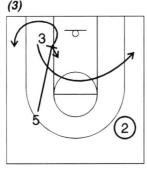

(3)

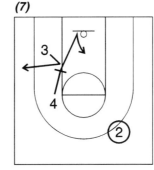

(7)

7. Vertical downscreen, fake up and fade: *Screener has opportunity to post up after he sets the screen.*

4. Weakside vertical backpick: *Low post weakside man sets vertical backscreen for weakside high post and steps out to the ball. High post cutter looks for the lob, or buttonhooks and posts for the ball in the lane.*

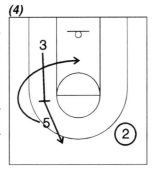

(4)

Diagrams to Demonstrate Each Move
Big men screening across or up the lane either horizontally or vertically

The big men must read their defenders. They can reverse pivot and go baseline to screen away, pivot over the top to screen away and even turn, fake the screen and immediately turn back to the ball to take advantage of defensive anticipation. Each move is tremendous and almost guarantees easy baskets.

The recipient of the screen must be alert, fake, and set up his defender and cut to the most openly advantageous area to enable him to receive the ball or to make the defense hesitate which will create a scoring opportunity for the offense.

It's also important to note that the screen across coming from the back side of the strongside post man is very difficult to defend. Most teams don't practice very much against this maneuver because few teams use it.

1. Screen across over the top and turn back opposite the cutter.

2. Turn baseline to screen and then pivot opposite the cutter. (The screener's pivot and turn is determined by the side his defender plays. If the defender is sealed, pass him the basketball!!!)

(1)

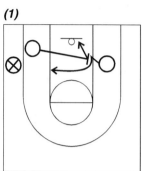

(2)

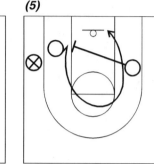

(3)

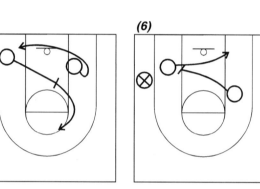

(4)

(5)

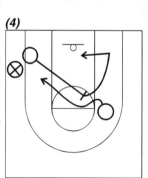

(6)

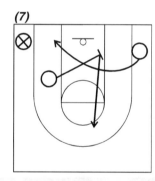

(7)

(8)

3. *Diagonal screen up and away:* On the baseline cut, the screener steps out to create space and a better passing lane.

4. *Screen away diagonally and cut over the top:* Here the screener circles back to the baseline, if open.

5. *Backscreen from the weak side, reverse pivot over the top:* The screener moves to the open area.

6. Backscreen, baseline cut and screener posts.

7. *Unbalanced set to establish a better angle:* Reverse pivot over the top. Set a screen and turn and move or cut to the open area.

8. Low-to-high diagonal backpick for a lob with the screener stepping out.

***The dribbler must create a good passing angle and screener must always see the ball to create space, passing lanes and passing options.

Coach's Edge

The aim of most defenses is to limit or stop the reversal of the ball. Work hard to make your players aware of this concept. We have devised methods to help them more easily reverse the ball. Continually drill and emphasize setting backscreens, running backdoors by moving without the ball and making weakside cuts. We try to emphasize the following in our drilling:

- Screeners should realize they can screen their own defenders to eliminate defensive switches.
- Continually look for opportunities to pick the picker and/or set more than one screen.
- Passers must not stand still after delivering a pass. They must cut, screen, spot-up, or fake and fade.
- Each time we receive the ball we want to establish the triple threat position to best see the floor.
- Screens may either be downscreens, back-picks or sidescreens. Call out the name of the player for whom the screen is set.
- Each offensive move is predicated on the understanding of the importance of reading the defense.
- Constantly emphasize timing, spacing, execution and moving without the ball.
- Rebound offensively.
- You must penetrate the opponent's defense.
- Searching for and taking high-percentage shots is a prime consideration. Don't inhibit your players, but make them understand the difference between a good and a bad shot.

7
Drilling Concepts and Teaching Points

Every coach has his own way of doing things. Our philosophy of drilling players has evolved through both trial and error and incorporating the ideas and drills of other coaches whose practices we have watched and also through participation, attendance and conversation at various basketball camps and clinics. I have also received tremendous input in devising drills from a number of valued close friends, assistant coaches and former players.

Begin by practicing each specific drill without the defense to familiarize the players with the spacing, timing and faking necessary for optimum offensive execution. Then walk through each movement against a defense before graduating to 2-on-2, 3-on-3, 4-on-4 and finally 5-on-5 game situations. In each drill rotate the players clockwise going from offense to defense, playing and defending each position on the floor.

We emphasize:

- Faking without the ball to establish position.
- Changing speed and direction.
- Being late rather than early when using screens.
- Establishing eye contact with the player with the ball to improve communication and create good passing angles.

Complete each drill by playing until the offense scores or the defense secures the basketball. Until the defense is successful, only rotate the offensive players which forces them to execute against the type of intensity they'll see in a game.

Then go a step farther. Permit the defense to fast break once it secures a rebound or intercepts the ball. Here, once again, you are able to concentrate on offensive rebounding, floor balance and defensive transition.

In our drills, our big men normally play every spot or position with the exception of the point, and we alternate sides of the floor. Once in awhile we permit our bigger players to play the point to help them better understand how important it is to help the ball handler by establishing good passing angles. This also increases their understanding of how hard the passer's job really is.

Coach's Edge

A useful practice tool is a clipboard or set of index cards to use to help players visualize and look at the particular play you want to run. Football coaches use this method and it works in basketball as well. With this method, the defense won't know which play you are going to run and will have to play honest defense against the play.

Coach's Edge

A good habit to establish before beginning each practice is to use the bulletin board in the dressing room to emphasize three points to concentrate on in that day's practice. Go over all three points with your team once you get together on the floor to reinforce this emphasis.

In recent years, the screen-and-roll has assumed a much larger role in offensive basketball. It's no longer used simply for last-second or final-shot situations, but widely used in the transition and half-court offenses. Where and how it's used, and whether it's from the top of the key, elbows, wings, corners or middle depends on each coach's philosophy, the ballhandling skills of his players and his confidence in their ability to shoot the three-point shot. It helps considerably if both the screener and dribbler are threats from beyond the arc.

Make sure your team is well-versed in the different options of the two-man game because teams constantly come up with new defensive schemes to stop it. Drill your players in how to handle the aggressive double-team, the hedge, a man fighting over or under, and the team that forces you to the middle, sideline or baseline. Your players must recognize each defense and be prepared to run plays in reaction to each defensive option or type of coverage they encounter.

Our players are taught how to set a screen facing the ball handler or with their backs to the dribbler. They also learn when to hold, split, step back or reset the screen and how to stretch and move the defense through use of the dribble. They are constantly reminded to look for the three-point shot if the defenders sag and to always look for penetrating angles when screens are set. Coaching in Europe has showed me how effective the fake, screen and go maneuver was in keeping the defense off balance.

We want the dribbler to be able to turn the corner and penetrate or flex the defense like an accordion. We use the screener step-back principle and want our players to automatically react when the defense traps and rotates from the weak side. Our receivers off the ball must recognize when and how to step into the gap and establish passing lanes for the man being double-teamed, minimizing good defensive recovery and rotation, and also how to cut from the weak side to split the defense. Our players are constantly reminded that always being able to see the ball of offense will give them confidence in destroying pressure defenses.

Our objective is to stretch, split, pop-out, turn the corner, reverse dribble and look to create mismatches by forcing the big man to defend on the perimeter. This takes him away from the boards and enhances our ability to rebound offensively. Our players are prepared to react to the defense that forces us to the middle and the defense that may try to force us to the sideline.

The screener and the passer are dangerous offensive players. The screener can read the defense and step back to the ball to get a shot when the defense reacts to stop or slow down the cutter. The passer can always take advantage of the defense once he has passed the ball. Both of these offensive players are in great position to create scoring opportunities for themselves or for teammates.

Shooters should realize that they are the most dangerous offensive rebounders once they shoot. Cutters must realize that if they cut off of a screen, stop, return and set a backpick, they are then able to step back and receive an easy shot opportunity.

We look to set diagonal backscreens, multiple and staggered screens, and try to teach our players not to be satisfied by setting one screen on a given play, but to continue to set another if possible. They must also recognize whether our opponents switch on equals or stay on equals and if they switch on all crosses with or without the ball.

Characteristics of a Successful Offensive Play

1. Obtain a good shot for a good shooter in a comfortable area and position on the court.

2. Big and small men in triangles with weakside and defensive balance positions should the shooter miss.

3. Make players aware of each other's strengths and tendencies.

4. Make players aware of where most offensive rebounds land or bounce to have a better chance of grabbing them and converting them to easy scores.

5. Make shooters aware of the fact that they are the most dangerous offensive rebounders because they know where the ball is going to land.

6. Ability to penetrate the defense.

7. Options should the defense stop our initial move.

Coach's Edge

A player who knows how to read and use screens is an integral part of a successful offense; more so if he is a shooter. Many outstanding college and professional players have made wonderful livings because they were pure shooters and were able to read screens. Many can't dribble to penetrate or create a shot, but their coaches wouldn't trade them for the world because of their ability to shoot the basketball which covers up many deficiencies.

Coach's Edge

Combat defensive switching by having the offensive players learn to split their defenders. Teach them to cut to the basket forcing the defensive players to make quick decisions concerning which man they should cover.

Breakdown Drills for Teaching the Screen-and-Roll

1. Try to always screen a defender, either your own or the man defending the man with the ball.

2. Set screens at a right angle to the defender, or with one foot directly behind him so the offensive man can fake and run him into the screen.

1. High post screen to wing: *Player with the ball may dribble in either direction depending on defensive pressure once the screen has been set. Here the screener cuts to the basket once the dribbler passes him with the ball.*

(1)

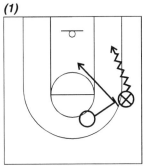

(3)

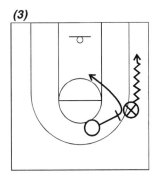

3. Quick release by the screener: *The screener moves to set a screen but instead cuts before the defense is set, anticipates or overcommits.*

2. Stepback by the screener: *After the dribbler penetrates, the screener steps back as an outlet or a shooter.*

(2)

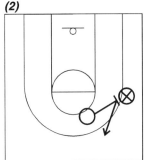

(4)

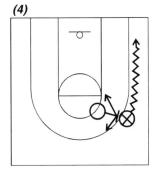

4. Force to sideline: *Set the screen-and-roll and/or step back or fade to receive as outlet or scoring threat.*

Screener options:

1. Roll to the basket on the penetration.

2. Step back on a switch or trap.

3. Split the defense before you actually stop and set the screen. (Fake the screen, turn to the basket and then roll.)

4. Set the screen either facing the ball handler or with your back to him.

5. Screen and screen again.

6. Fake the cutaway, return and screen.

7. Handback and screen.

8. Reverse pivot and screen.

Breakdown Drills for Teaching the Screen-and-Roll

1. Baseline to wing screen-and-roll: *Coming up from low post to set a screen on the defender. Screener sets a right-angle screen either facing or with his back to the man he is screening.*

(1)
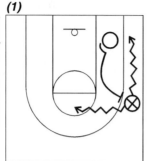

(5)
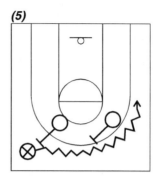

5. Double high post staggered screen-and-roll: *Successive blind staggered screens for the point man are set by the high post players. Dribbler may penetrate after either screen, cross over and/or reverse dribble and penetrate.*

2. High post or elbow down to screen in the corner: *Screener is taught to roll with the force of the blow as he makes contact with the man he screens once the dribbler passes him.*

(2)
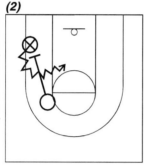

(6)
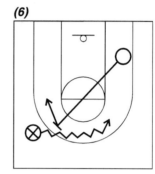

6. Diagonal screen up and across: *Blind diagonal screen from a distance causing the defenders to cover much more space making their help options more difficult.*

3. Low post to corner screen: *Offensive low post player leaves his position and steps out to the corner to screen the man defending man with the ball. This also aids us when we teach low post men to also step out and screen players without the ball.*

(3)
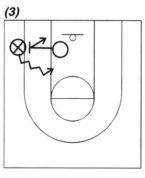

(7)
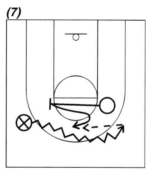

7. *Screen once and then screen again once the dribbler has passed you and changed his direction or speed to open up the court.*

8. High screen across from opposite high post to wing: *The screener's defender must again cover distance and the man with the ball has most of the court available for penetration. However, the dribbler must wait until the screener is stationary before penetrating to avoid committing an offensive foul.*

4. Elbow to top of the key: *High post man steps up from behind to screen the defender on the ball. He sets a blind screen and then uses his screening options.*

(4)
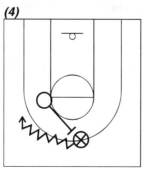

(8)
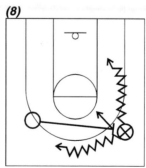

Diagrams to Demonstrate Each Offensive Move With and Without the Defense in Place

No Defense

Defense
Backdoor move

1. As X2 overplays 02 on the wing between the ball and his man, 1, the player with the ball, dribbles at the back leg of X2. This permits 2 the opportunity to execute a "V" cut behind his defender to the basket. In this situation the best pass is a bounce pass from 1 to 2.

(1A)

(1B)

Backdoor move with a flash post

2. Player 5 recognizes that X2 is between his man and the ball in an overplaying position to prevent the pass from 1. To free his teammate, 5 breaks high and from an angle to the ball and a pass from 1, then executes a backdoor bounce pass to 2 who has faked his defender towards 1 and cuts behind him to the basket. Timing is the key in this play. 2 can't cut backdoor until 1 has passed to 5.

(2A)

(2B)

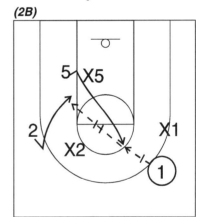

Coach's Edge

Once we begin practicing against a live defense we establish a rule that the defense must remain on the court until it successfully stops the offense from scoring. If the offense scores, we rotate our offensive players, not the defenders. They stay on the court until they have attained a defensive "stop."

Diagrams to Demonstrate Each Offensive Move
With and Without the Defense in Place

No Defense   **Defense**

1A. Buttonhook:
4 on the wing fakes toward the basket and breaks out to the wing area to receive a pass from 1. After making the pass, 1 "V" fakes away from the ball and comes back outside of 4 to receive a return or handback pass.

(1A)

(1B)

1B. 1 passes to 4 breaking out to the wing after 4 has faked X4 to the goal. After passing the ball, 1 moves his man away and quickly cuts outside of 4 for a return pass (handback).

2A. 4 hands the ball back to 1 and cuts directly to the goal and into the middle of the lane keeping his body between the ball and his defender. He then stops and pivots back to the ball sealing his defender behind him.

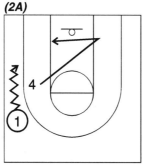

(2A)

(2B)

2B. After 4 hands the ball back to 1 he cuts to the basket, gets his defender in front of him under the goal and quickly turns and pivots back to the ball sealing his defender behind him. The direction of his pivot is determined by the position of his defender, enabling him to establish the best position to receive a pass and score.

3A. Buttonhook with dribble entry:
1 dribbles the sideline as 4 in the low post turns and begins to screen away across the lane and again keeps his man in front of him. He crosses under the goal, stops, pivots over or under to the ball and sealing his defender behind him to receive the pass in excellent scoring position.

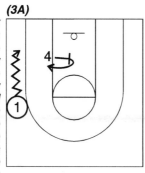

(3A)

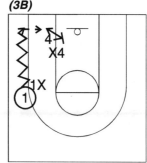

(3B)

3B. Here 4 executes a front pivot across his body and seals his defender toward the foul line. 4 can then execute a sit-down or drop-step move to the baseline.

72

Diagrams to Demonstrate Each Offensive Move
With and Without the Defense in Place

No Defense   **Defense**

1A. "L" cut following handback: *3 on the wing "V" fakes his defender to the basket and comes back to meet the pass from 1, then hands ball back to 1 when he cuts behind him. After the handback, 3 takes two or three steps away from 1 parallel to the baseline, cuts down the lane to basket.*

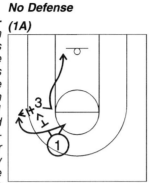

(1A)

(1B)

1B. *Following the 3-to-1 handback, the parallel cut enables 3 to freeze X3 in front of him permitting him a quick cut down the free-throw lane with his defender sealed behind him where he is in position to receive a pass and score.*

2A. *3 executes an "L" cut after he sets a screen on 1 to use to penetrate to the basket.*
2B. *After 1 passes to 3, he fakes away before returning for*

the handback. This denies X1 the opportunity to step into the passing lane to deter the handback.
2C. *Following the second pass, 3 cuts horizontally in front of X3*

and then executes a right-angle vertical cut to the basket to seal his (X3) from the ball. If he is able to do this, 1 cuts directly backdoor and to the basket.

(2A)

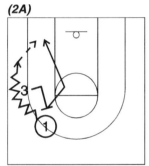

(2B)

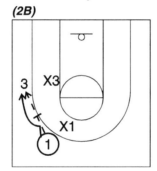

(2C)

(3A)

(3B)

3A. *"V" cut executed after 1 passes the ball to 3 on the wing. He fakes one way and then cuts the other way in order to free himself by moving his defender in the opposite direction.*

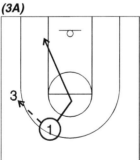

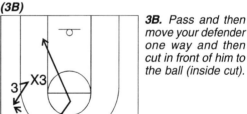

3B. *Pass and then move your defender one way and then cut in front of him to the ball (inside cut).*

(4A)

(4B)

4A. *"V" cut executed by 3 in order to move his man and receive the ball in position to turn and face the basket.*

4B. *1 passes to 3, fakes to the ball and cuts around X1 instead of in front of him because X1 is trying to deny him the ball. An example of 1 "reading the defense."*

Diagrams to Demonstrate Each Offensive Move
With and Without the Defense in Place

No Defense   **Defense**

1A. Weakside cut to the ball: *2 takes advantage of the helping defense off ball by reading the defense and cutting to strong side when his defender turns his head to watch ball or turns his back. Players are taught to cut behind their man to the basket if the defender shows his back.*

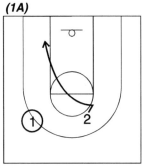
(1A)

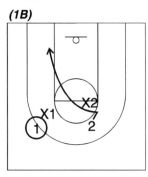
(1B)

1B. *The cut of the weakside offensive player to the strong or ball side depends on reading the defense and faking the defender to set up the most efficient cut to the basket.*

2A. *If the defense off the ball tries to help, the offensive post man cuts behind or backdoors his defender to the goal. A fine example of reading the defense and communicating with a teammate to set up a successful two-man play.*

(2A)

(2B)

2B. *The man without the ball first fakes to move his defender and then closes the distance between himself and his defender, forcing him to honor the move. This helps eliminate the support or helping defense.*

3A. Shuffle Cut: *3 uses a weakside elbow or higher screen set by 5, fakes his man away and "V" cuts to the basket from the weak side.*

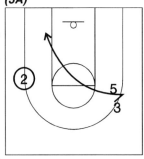
(3A)

(3B)

3B. *On the shuffle cut, the man cutting goes over or under the screen depending on how the defender plays him and the ball.*

4A. Flex cut: *Baseline cut from weak side to strong side across the lane or on the baseline as ball is reversed. If 1 has ball, the cut by 3 is from the strong side. When 2 has the ball, cut comes from the weak side. Proper timing is important on this cut.* **Cut late instead of early when using a screen.**

(4A)

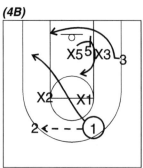
(4B)

4B. *On the flex cut, the cutter's route depends on how the defense plays him. On both cuts, if the screener's defender switches to the cutter, the screener can step to the ball for a pass and easy scoring opportunity.*

Diagrams to Demonstrate Each Offensive Move
With and Without the Defense in Place

No Defense   **Defense**

Give-and-Go

(1A) 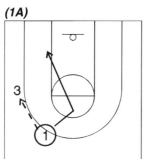   *(1B)*

1A. We utilize the "V" cut, inside cut or fake a change of direction to go around the defender. We use this a great deal when the passer's defender moves into the passing lane once the pass is made.

1B. The give-and-go cut is also often described as the pass-and-cut. The passer is looking for a quick return pass when his defender turns his head to look at the ball.

(2A) 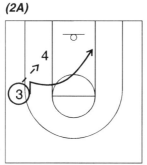   *(2B)*

2A. A very important counter play when, on a pass to the low post, the passer's defender traps the low post man.

2B. 3 passes to the low post and cuts down the lane or spots in the corner depending on how his defender turns to see the ball or trap the low post.

Handback

3A. Point passes to the wing and after faking his defender, follows the ball to receive a return pass from the wing.

Pinch post handback

(3A)    *(3B)*

4A. Post man is outside the elbow area and the passer's defender is not able to see the ball or the man who has it unless he turns his head.

3B. The handback option is used to keep the ball in the point guard's hands against sluffing defenses.

****Probably the most important point in executing the pinch post is the post man faking his defender toward the lane and the post cutting parallel up the lane to seal his man and receive the ball which relieves defensive pressure to create open offensive space.

(4A) 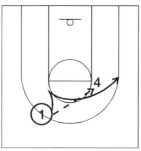   *(4B)*

4B. A good entry pass when the defense pressures the point guard and when we are able to flash post to the elbow area from the baseline or wing areas.

Diagrams to Demonstrate Each Offensive Move
With and Without the Defense in Place

No Defense | **Defense**

(1A) **(1B)**

1. Dribble clearout: *The player with the ball dribbles to an area and the offensive man in that area moves to another position on the court clearing the area for the man with the ball. We instruct our players to always see the ball on offense to enable them to determine if the defense attempts to double-team or trap the ball. Our offensive player must be in a position to provide a passing outlet and lane for the player being trapped or pressured.*

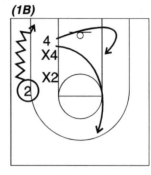

Provides a one-on-one opportunity for the player with the ball as his teammate moves or cuts to another area. We again emphasize that the cutter must see the ball.

(1C) **(1D)**

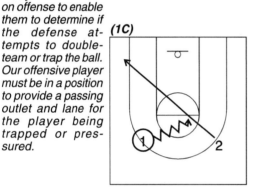
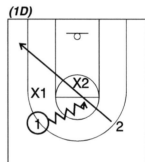

** Should the defense switch onto or jump 1, 2 is in a position to receive a return pass if he follows our rule of always being able to see the ball on offense as well as on defense.

(2A) **(2B)**

2. Flare move: *1 passes the ball and then uses a back or sidescreen from the other direction to rub off his defender, freeing himself for a return pass to use to either shoot or simply to move the defense.*

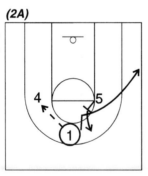

*On the flare to the weak side without the ball, 2 reads the defense and gets free by using the weakside screen. He has the option of cutting **over or under** the screen depending on how his defender plays the cut.*

(2C) **(2D)**

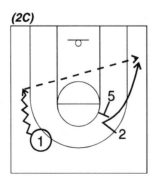

Diagrams to Demonstrate Each Offensive Move
With and Without the Defense in Place

No Defense   *Defense*

(1A)   **(1B)**

High-Low

1A. Pass from the high post inside to the low post on the block or in the paint with the defender sealed behind or on the side of the offensive low post man.

1B. Pass from high to low post with low post defender fronting or playing 3-4 on the side of the low post. The low post man is in a position to receive a pass inside from the high post which takes away the help from the other big man. We also use this when we have created a mismatch situation.

(2A)   **(2B)**

2. Example of the high-low when the low post is fronted.

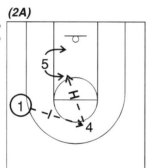

(3A)   **(3B)**

3A. The low post man has sealed his defender and the ball is reversed to the high post who passes the ball inside from the top of the key. Emphasizes the importance of our big people being able to pass the ball.

3B. The low post being defended in a three-quarter position with the ball on the wing.

Mismatch
4A. When X1 and X3 have switched on the wing to baseline pin down on the UCLA wing pass to the high post to reverse the ball and look inside when the defender is sealed or fronting and therefore not able to stop a lob pass inside.

4B. When X1 has switched with X3 and he is fronting 3 on the low post, the wing reverses the ball to the high post as 3 seals the defender on his back to better receive a pass inside the free-throw lane.

Diagrams to Demonstrate Each Offensive Move With and Without the Defense in Place

Inside Handoff

Used against sluffing defenses and when the passer's cutter has a tendency to relax once his man passes the ball. This is also a surprise move we use when the defense also tries to overplay and deny the handback. 1 has a direct cutting line to the basket.

No Defense   **Defense**

(1A)   **(1B)**

1A. *1 passes the ball to 3 on the wing and fakes a step to the outside and then cuts directly inside of 3 to receive a direct handoff as he cuts to the basket.*

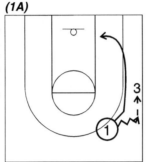 

1B. *1 passes and cuts inside both defenders after first faking to the sideline. This play was used a great deal by the Boston Celtics as a surprise move on the transition.*

(2A)   **(2B)**

2A. Isolation: *Clear all defenders away from the ball by screening them, if possible, to permit the man with the ball the opportunity to take his defender one-on-one.*

2B. *Clearout or isolation situation for 4 from the elbow or high post.*

(3A)   **(3B)**

3A. Lob pass or alley-oop: *Clear out a side and pass over the defender after the weakside backpick versus pressure.*

 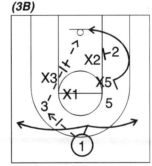

3B. Lob or alley-oop pass resulting in a layup or a slam dunk: *We look for this move and pass when the weakside high post is being pressured and denied.*

(4A)   **(4B)**

4A. *Weakside back-pick to set up the lob pass.*

4B. *Especially effective when screener's defender chases the screener or a small man switches to defend a taller opponent.*

Diagrams to Demonstrate Each Offensive Move
With and Without the Defense in Place

No Defense   **Defense**

1A. Misdirection screening: *Using a blind backpick from the weak side to free a player away from the ball.*

(1A)

(1B)

1B. Screening defenders away from ball: *Attacking the defense from behind or from the weak side. We also use this to take advantage of the mismatch when the defense switches. 2 can screen X2 to free 5.*

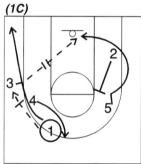
(1C)

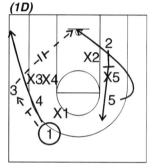
(1D)

3A. Pick-and-roll, screen-and-roll or two-man game: *Normally used by two players of different size with the smaller of the two controlling the ball. This, however, may depend on the skill of the players involved.*

(3A)

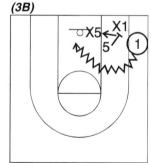
(3B)

3B. *Designed to create penetration, to force the defense to switch, cause indecision and mismatches. We use this in many different areas of the court depending on the defense and the skills of our players.*

4A. *Man setting the screen has option of rolling to the basket, stepping back or splitting the defense. Screen may be set on the elbow, high post or wing.*

(4A)

(4B)

4B. *The man without the ball normally sets the screen, but not always. We can also use this from our pinch post and handback options.*

Diagrams to Demonstrate Each Offensive Move With and Without the Defense in Place

No Defense   **Defense**

(1A)   **(1B)**

1. Screening for the man with the ball from the wing to the point: *Screen is executed by the wing on the side of and at a right angle with the ball handler's defensive man.*

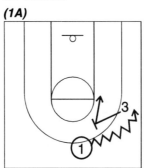

****Remember, it's great basketball when smaller players screen for bigger players because the defense must make a decision to switch, stay, bump, body check, hedge, trap or stay. Each adjustment means a new decision and a risk of making a costly mistake not easily corrected.*

(2A)   **(2B)**

2A. Big men screening across the lane: *4 pivots away from the ball and across the lane to screen for 5. The player waiting for the screen should fake and move his man but he should not cut off of the screen until the screen has been set.*

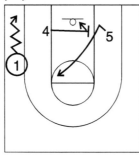

2B. *The man nearest the ball turns and screens horizontally across the lane. Once there, he waits for his teammate to cut and then seals his defender and pivots in the direction opposite the cutter providing an option for the passer if the first cutter is not free or if the defense switches.*

(3A)   **(3B)**

3A. *Backpicks to set up the flare or fade move and subsequent skip pass. The skip pass is normally described as a crosscourt pass or a pass to the wing area which passes over two defenders to the other side of the court.*

3B. *We use this move when the defenders overplay to the ball side to help or to stop our penetration.*

(4A)   **(4B)**

4A. Vertical downscreens: *Zipper action describing the passing options available to the passer. 2 must wait for 4 to set the screen before moving.*

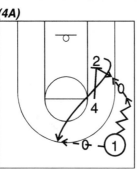

4B. *Example of the different uses of screens.*

Diagrams to Demonstrate Each Offensive Move
With and Without the Defense in Place

No Defense   **Defense**

(1A)   **(1B)**

1A: Sidepick or sidescreen: *Used from the weak side away from the ball to combat close high post pressure and set up the high lob via a reverse cut to the basket. The screener then steps out as an outlet after he sets the screen.*

Blind horizontal screen from the weak side.

(2A)   **(2B)**

2A. Staggered double or triple screens: *Successive screens, one after the other, instead of shoulder-to-shoulder which cause defenders to fight through more than one screen making switching more difficult.*

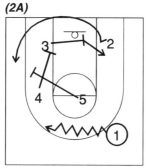
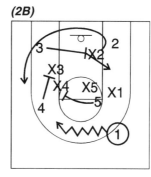

2B. *We cause the defenders to fight through successive screens over a greater area of the court and this makes switching of equals difficult and also permits us to post up and step to the ball on switches.*

(3A)   **(3B)**

3A. Slash screening and brush blocking diagonally across and around the high post or free-throw line area: *Can be accomplished with either the man nearest the ball or the man away from the ball making the initial cut.*

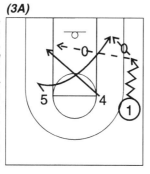

3B. *We can also use this by our backcourt players with the ball on the wing or high post. The man setting the screen depends on how the defense plays.*

(4A)   **(4B)**

4A. Multiple screens: *The same player sets more than one screen on the same play. They can be front, side or backscreens, staggered or misdirection.*

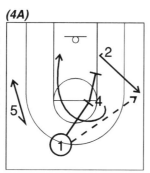

4B. *We can set possibly a double and then a single screen. We feel this is a much more efficient use of our cutters without the ball and that it also creates greater movement and passing and cutting options.*

Diagrams to Demonstrate Each Offensive Move
With and Without the Defense in Place

No Defense

Defense

(1A)

(1B)

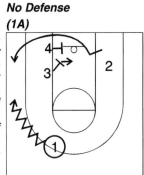

1A. Double shoulder-to-shoulder screens: *Option to use when you want a wider screen instead of a staggered one. Can be set on the baseline, top of the key, foul line and/or outside the elbow area.*

1B. *The baseline cutter can fake before he reaches the screen or just when he is next to it. He may also cut out of bounds and then step in to give him more room and give the screeners better angles in which to screen his defender.*

(2A)

(2B)

2A. Triple screen: *Normally used on the side of the free-throw lane. It's frequently used in under-the-basket out-of-bounds situations.*

2B. *In our offensive philosophy, we also encourage screeners to screen their respective defenders to make switching and fighting through much more difficult.*

(3A)

(3B)

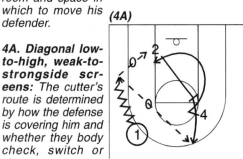

3A. Double baseline staggered screen inside the paint: *Sometimes the man we are screening for waits on the other side of the lane until both players are almost on the weak side before he cuts. This gives him more room and space in which to move his defender.*

3B. *Screeners coming across the lane.*

(4A)

(4B)

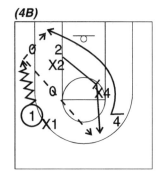

4A. Diagonal low-to-high, weak-to-strongside screens: *The cutter's route is determined by how the defense is covering him and whether they body check, switch or stay.*

4B. *2 may first screen X2 to prevent the switch and then continue by screening X4.*

Diagrams to Demonstrate Each Offensive Move With and Without the Defense in Place

No Defense   **Defense**

Diagonal downscreens from the weak to the strong side

(1A)   **(1B)**

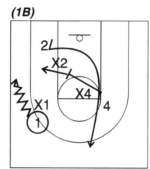

1A. Here we screen big to small but we invert our players and also screen small to big in certain situations if our big man is an offensive threat from this area or if we want to post a player.

1B. In this diagonal screening action we again encourage 2 to wait until the screen has been set before moving. This gives him different options and we also tell him he may cut inside or outside depending on how the defense plays the screen.

Stacks

(2A)   **(2B)**

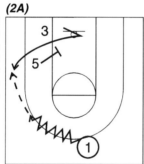

2A. Normally set along the lane. We also diagonally stagger our stacks which gives us a better screening angle whether we screen down or screen up.

2B. Either the top man or bottom man can set the screen but this depends on the location of the ball and whether the defense inverts the defenders or plays straight up.

Curl, loop or circle

(3A)   **(3B)**

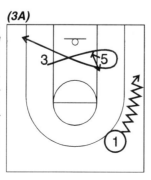

3A. 3 moves across the lane to 5 and cuts under and then over 5 as be uses him as a screener. 3 can free himself by this cut by rubbing his man off of 5 or he can cause 5's man to cover him which then frees 5 in the low post.

3B. 5 is responsible for screening X3 or X5. This depends on how the defense reacts. He must read the defense and then decide who to screen.

Diagrams to Demonstrate Each Offensive Move With and Without the Defense in Place

No Defense   **Defense**

Triangle action

(1A)   **(1B)**

1A. First we set one horizontal screen across the lane, then a vertical downscreen for the shooter in the pick-the-picker principle. In this situation we may also use one backscreen and one downscreen or mix the screens in any way we wish.

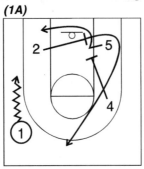
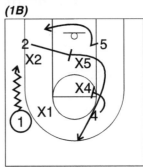

1B. Baseline man receiving the screen has the option to cut in either direction. He must decide which provides the best scoring opportunity. 4 also has the option of screening his own defender as do all of our players in similar situations.

(2A)   **(2B)**

2. Example of utilizing two backscreens.

Turnouts

(3A)   **(3B)**

Our normal rule is that the man on the ball side sets the screen for the other cutter, but we can change this via communication between our cutters.

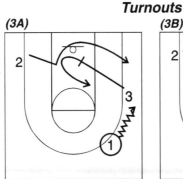

Explanation of cutter and screener with their defenders.

Turnout cutter options

(4)

4. 2 may circle the screener, cut to the corner, turn and go up to the elbow along the lane or circle and go diagonally across and up in the direction of the opposite elbow. He may set a screen on any of his cuts.

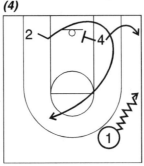

Diagrams to Demonstrate Each Offensive Move With and Without the Defense in Place

No Defense **Defense**

(1A) (1B)

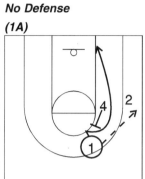 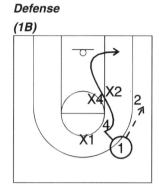

1A. UCLA vertical screen: High post steps up and sets a backscreen for the point man after the point passes to the wing and cuts down the lane. He may cut inside or around the high post depending on how he is played by his defender.

1B. Cuts showing the defense in certain positions in relation to the ball.

(2A) (2B)

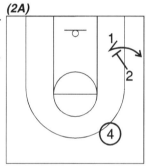 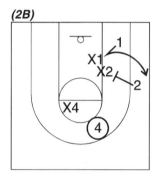

2. UCLA backpick or pindown after the wing passes to the high post stepping out providing 1 was not free for a return pass after his cut.

(3A) (3B)

 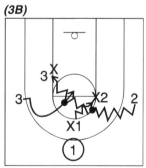

3A. Weave action with the dribble: Three men dribbling, handing off, interchanging and screening using penetration to get to the basket.

3B. The players dribbling try to screen the opposition's defenders on the dribble exchange. It's the responsibility of the receiver to set up his man so that the angle when he receives the handoff is a penetrating one and the dribbler should face the basket and keep his body between the ball and his defender. He should also dribble at the back leg of the receiver's defender to set a right-angle screen.

(4A) (4B)

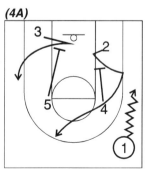 

4. Zipper moves: Vertical screen with ball on the weak side. Best shooter normally begins on the baseline, but with backscreens and misdirection this is not always the case today.

85

8
Out-of-Bounds Plays

Sideline Plays

Each coach must decide what his goal is when running normal out-of-bounds plays along the sidelines whether on the full court, from three-quarter court or any place over the half-court line in the attacking zone. This is a coach's major philosophical decision.

We aren't speaking here of situations at the end of a period or game when you need to score in order to win, but rather any time the ball is inbounded following a foul, turnover, deflection, time-out or technical foul.

First decide whether you simply want to inbound the ball safely and run a set play, or your motion or delay game offense. Or are you looking for a quick score by running a play on every out-of-bounds possession?

The latter is more advantageous. It puts pressure on the defense by not allowing it to relax, get set, or think about the score or game situation.

Every coach is a student of the game, and we study the great coaches and teams. The Boston Celtics under the legendary Red Auerbach ran many of their out-of-bounds plays for the inbounds passer, usually their most prolific offensive player. It's a tactic Celtics coaches still use. Why change if it's successful?

My philosophy is to always look to score in these situations.

Auerbach's rationale is well-founded because it usually places the opposition's best defender on the inbounds passer, putting him at a disadvantage because he is unable to both pressure the ball and locate his opponent's offensive teammates. Therefore, he has almost no idea where the receivers or screeners are coming from, and his decision of whether to pressure the pass or sluff off and bump the passer after he releases the ball is more difficult.

This hurts his ability to anticipate or trap and diminishes his value as his team's best defender. He has to concentrate solely on the inbounds passer who normally is the most dangerous player on the floor, not only because he is a great scorer but also because he has a better opportunity to take advantage of the weaknesses in the defense and set up his man to receive the ball in prime shooting range and position.

The box offense is easy to run in these situations because many of the cuts, screens and passes are consistent with our teaching philosophy and methods. We are able to read the defense and establish similar passing angles and outlet opportunities. The passers learn to handle pressure and make good, sound decisions.

Each play has alternatives or options, but the players know that even though we try to score every time we have a side out-of-bounds situation unless we specifically have a reason not to, their most important responsibility is to inbound the ball safely. Then we can retain control if we immediately intend to attack the defense.

Inbounds passers should count off five seconds to themselves when they receive the ball from the referee because it's difficult to see the other nine players. Tell the passer to step back from the sideline to get better passing angles and a clearer view of the court when inbounding under pressure from the defender.

Make sure the passer understands that he can use the full five seconds when inbounding. Many defenses relax once the offense makes its initial cut after the official hands the ball to the offensive player. Players should exercise patience and confidence in these situations. They need to understand how long five seconds really takes and what can be accomplished in this short period of time.

Players should hustle to their spots but not step out of bounds to receive the ball until everyone is ready. Try to persuade the official to hand the ball over when your players want it even though the defense may not be prepared.

Coaches decide how and when to call signals for out-of-bounds plays and when to inbound the ball. Signal or call the plays before the player steps out of bounds to receive the ball from the referee and try to have someone repeat the signal or key to make certain every offensive player is ready. Decide what key to use to begin a play. Each player should move once the inbounding player slaps the ball, gives a verbal signal, bounces the ball, holds it over his head with two hands or as soon as the ball leaves the official's hands.

Coach's Edge

Most defenders tend to relax if their man doesn't receive the ball after the first or second pass or following the first or second screen on out-of-bounds plays. This is when to take advantage of defensive lapses by constantly moving without the ball.

In the latter case, if players move when the ball is in the air, they actually have six or seven seconds to run the play instead of five because the timer is instructed to start the clock once the inbounds player has touched the ball. The defense reacts in much the same manner.

Don't forget the human element, however. Timekeepers usually favor the home team. When playing on the road, anything is likely to occur.

We have used Auerbach's philosophy in designing our side out-of-bounds plays and strategies because it gives our best offensive players as many scoring opportunities as possible during a game. We also steal a page from the Chicago Bulls' triple post offense devised by assistant coach Tex Winter when he coached at Kansas State by running our normal offense as an out-of-bounds play.

We run our half-court offense from the side out-of-bounds under normal conditions in practice every day against a live defense and in dummy situations to work on execution. Like the Bulls, our passer initiates the play as though the side position was the wing, corner or point position inside the court. All other positions and spacing are consistent with our normal offensive places on the court. Our movements may vary, but normally our cuts, fakes and screens are consistent.

The Celtic philosophy is taken a step further as the Bulls have done. Instead of simply deciding to have our best scorer or best passer inbound the ball, each player can successfully undertake this responsibility. Each is expected to make the pass and then run his man off of a screen, set a screen and/or cut, and receive a return pass in scoring position.

Big men are used to inbound the ball because they can see over the defense in need or last-second situations. It makes sound basketball sense to use this tactic to take our opponent's best defender out of the play. For example, the point guard will inbound and relieve the pressure he faces when the defense is geared to deny him the first pass in side out-of-bounds situations.

Coach's Edge

We practice every out-of-bounds or last-second situation beforehand so that the players understand their responsibilities. They are diagrammed again during time-outs to reinforce and help the players visualize what is to be done. They will be more confident in meeting the objectives if they have practiced them. They should never feel that what we are doing is a last-second decision that has neither been practiced nor prepared for. Confidence breeds success.

Using the point guard or any other player as the inbounder forces his defender to cover him after he passes. Not only is the point the best passer and decision maker, but the man guarding him is forced to defend in what may be an unnatural situation. The best passer can now also be used as a screener, cutter, receiver and decoy, if necessary. In side out-of-bounds situations, the nearer the passer is to the midcourt line, the higher the offensive players are placed inside the court. This eliminates extremely long and dangerous initial or crosscourt passes and provides an outstanding opportunity to take advantage of an opponent who uses pressure or an overplay defensive style. Conversely, certain plays or options should not be run near the corners of the court or the midcourt line to prevent opponents from using the sidelines, midcourt or endlines as additional defenders in these areas.

Another point often overlooked is that enabling and exposing different players to the responsibility of executing the inbounds pass makes them more aware of the difficulty of the task and reinforces each player's appreciation for establishing open and clearly visible lanes for the passer. This also prepares them for situations when key players are out because of injuries or personal fouls.

Coach's Edge

In the NBA, each team has seven time-outs per game. In addition, each team is allowed as many as four 20-second timeouts. These play stoppages, plus side out-of-bounds opportunities following the first four non-shooting fouls in each quarter, emphasize the importance of successful execution on side out-of-bounds situations. Each is a scoring opportunity which can place the defense at a disadvantage. Time-outs and side and under-the-basket opportunities occur at all levels of basketball although the number of opportunities varies at each level.

Coach's Edge

Anticipation or advance preparation is the coach's responsibility. Lack of preparation is a hollow excuse for losing a basketball game.

The smart coach prepares and takes maximum advantage of every scoring opportunity. Everyone wants to win a championship, and this is one way to put a team in position to reach that goal.

Side Out-of-Bounds Plays

1. Play is designed for the 3 man with secondary options: 4 inbounds the ball to 3 after 3 has run his defender into the double screen set by 1 and 5. 2 waits until 3 has cut and moves opposite the cut of 3 following 1 stepping out to the weakside wing area. 3 receives and has an immediate shot opportunity; if covered, 2 is our second option. If 2 makes the pass to 1 who has 5 posting low, 3 in this instance sets a backscreen for 4 or has 4 pin down for him. When we do reverse the ball, it's in the hands of our primary ball handler.

2. 3 is our inbounder. 5 screens down for 1 and 3 passes to 1. 5 pivots after his screen and is the secondary outlet. After passing, 3 receives a staggered double screen from 2 and 4 and continues to the opposite corner for a pass and a shooting opportunity. If 3 is not open, 1 can pass back to 2 who has received a pick from 5. 4 circles to the low post off of 5 on the play's continuity.

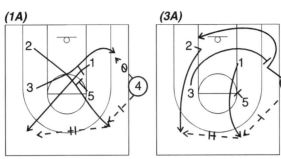

(1A)

(1B)

(2A)

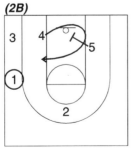

(2B)

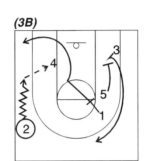

(3A)

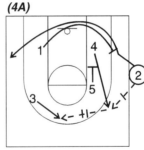

(3B)

(4A)

(4B)

3. Ball is inbounded by 4 with 1 and 2 on the baseline. 5 sets a screen for 1 who receives the pass as 3 diagonally picks down for 4 and 2 breaks to the weakside wing and a pass from 1 to look at 4 posting after cutting off of the screen by 3. When 2 has the ball his options are 4 posting low or a pass to 3 who has received a double staggered misdirection screen from 5 and 1. If 3 has no shot he looks to post 5 as 1 clears to the weak side of the court.

4. Double screen for 1. 2 inbounds the ball to 4 who has received a vertical zipper downscreen from 5. 1 crosses the lane to set a backscreen on the strongside block for 2 as 4 passes to 3 stepping out.

Once 3 receives the ball, 5 and 4 set a staggered double vertical screen for 1 coming up from the baseline.

Side Out-of-Bounds Plays

Plays 5 and 6 are examples of misdirection plays.

5A. Double screens: 1 inbounds the ball as 4 and 5 set a double screen for 2 coming high for the ball. 3 is the secondary outlet on the low block on the strong side. If 2 receives the pass, 3 sets a backscreen for 1 who cuts low after the pass.

5B. If 2 doesn't have a shooting or penetrating opportunity, he passes to 1 on the wing as 4 and 5 set a double screen for 3 circling into the lane. If 3 continues to the corner without the ball, 5 will circle into the lane around 4.

6A. 1 inbounds to 3 breaking up to the ball from the strongside low post as 4 and 5 vertically screen low on the weakside block for 2. 2 fakes up and cuts instead to the strongside wing for a pass as the secondary outlet.

6B. If 3 receives from 1, 2 sets a backscreen for 1 after the inbounds pass, and 4 and 5 cross the lane and set a double screen for 1 who continues to cut along the baseline.

(5A)

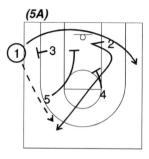

(5B)

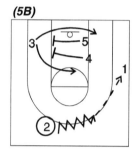

(6A)

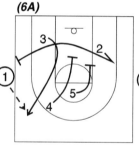

(6B)

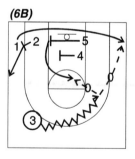

(7A)

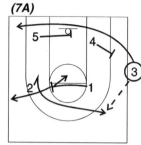

(7B)

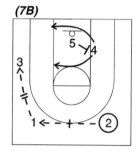

(8A)

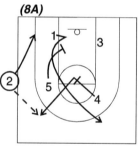

(8B)

7A. 3 inbounds as 1 horizontally screens across for 2. 4 is on the low block as an option if free. If the first pass is to 2, 4 and 5 set a staggered double baseline screen for 3 as 2 reverses the ball to 1 who has continued across the court and 1 looks for 3.

7B. When 3 receives, 1 screens and interchanges with 2, and 5 sets another screen for 4 circling back into the lane.

8A. Misdirection for inbounder 2 or double screen for 3 after inbounds pass to 4 and ball reversal to 1. Once 2 inbounds ball to 4 after 4 screens for 1, 2 cuts to low post and waits.

8B. On the pass from 4 to 1, 2 cuts baseline to the ball side off of a screen by 3 and 3 continues to screen 5 then continues off of a screen from 4 in pick-the-picker movement.

Side Out-of-Bounds Plays

(9A)

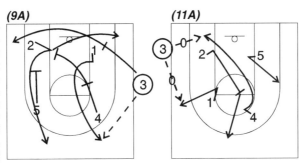

9A. *Zipper option or double screen for the 2 man as 3 inbounds the ball: 4 vertical pins down for 1 to receive the entry pass. 5 screens down for 2 once 1 has received the pass. If 1 is covered, 4 and 5 must see the ball as outlets.*

9B. *2 reads the defense on the inbounds pass to 1 and may cut up off the weakside zipper screen by 5 or fake this move and cut baseline off a staggered double screen set first by 4 and then 3. On this pass to 2, 3 and 4 pick 5 low.*

(9B)

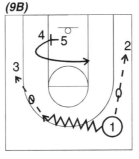

10A. Screen-and-roll, zipper and penetrate-and-pitch options: *3 inbounds to 1 breaking off of 5. When 1 receives, 4 picks down on 2 cutting high on the weakside zipper move. 3 cuts and clears baseline after his pass.*

(10A)

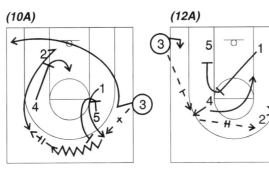

10B. *When 1 has received, 5 pivots and comes back to the ball and screens for 1. 4 posts low, 2 and 3 spot up and 1 and 5 now run the two-man game as 1 also looks to penetrate and/or pitch.*

(10B)

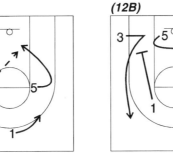

(11A)

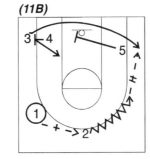

11A. Diagonal screen action: *3 inbounds the ball and looks to pass to 4 cutting low off of a diagonal screen from 2 from the strongside low post. 1 fakes and breaks out to draw the defense and help create a passing lane for 3. 1 is an outlet and 2 steps out after screening 4. The first option is 4 low; the second option is 1.*

11B. *If 1 receives, he looks for 2 who then looks to reverse the ball to 3 cutting baseline off a screen by 5 who pivots and posts after the screen.*

(11B)

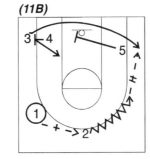

(12A)

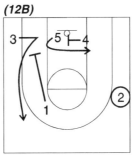

12A. Diagonal small-on-big continuity after the inbounds pass from 3 to 4 stepping out: *The first option is 3 passing to 5 on the low post; the second option is to 4 and then 4 to 2.*

12B. *When 2 receives, 1 diagonally screens up for 4 cutting to the low block. After the pick for 4, 1 pivots and screens down for 3 on the weak side.*

(12B)

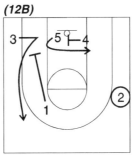

Side Out-of-Bounds Plays

(13A)

13A. Zipper: *3 inbounds and looks to pass to 1 who waits on the baseline for a vertical downscreen from 5. 3 passes to 1 if he is free, or to 5 posting low. Once 1 has the ball, 4 downscreens for 2, breaking up for the pass from 1 for an open shot as 4 pivots to post.*

13B. *Once 2 receives, 1 screens away for 3 or 3 fakes up and cuts along the baseline off of 5 and 4 to the ball side for the ball. 2 now has a number of options.*

(13B)

(15A)

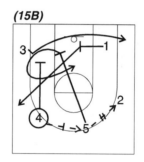

15A. Downscreen, flare and misdirection options: *3 inbounds to 4 after 4 has screened down on 2 from the elbow to the low block and 2 has used a sidescreen by 5 and flared to the weak side of the court. 4 passes to 5 and 5 reverses the ball to 2.*

15B. *Once 2 receives the ball, 1, who has remained on the low block, crosses the lane and he and 5 screen across for 3. On continuity, 4 and 5 screen down on the weak side for 1, then both post on the blocks.*

(15B)

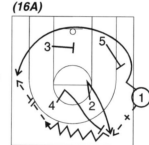

14A. Crossing action with pick-the-picker continuity: *3 inbounds to 5 stepping out as 1 screens across for 2 on the baseline. 3 also picks for 2 after making the pass to 5.*

(14A)

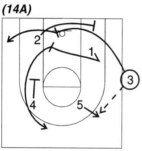

(16A)

16A. Screen-and-roll and baseline screens: *1 inbounds to 2 and cuts away opposite the ball. Once 2 receives the ball, 4 comes up and sets a backscreen for him. 2 drives off of pick by 4; 5 and 3 set baseline screens for 1. 2 can penetrate or pass to 1.*

14B. *5 has the option of passing to 2 cutting or continuing to the corner, or to 1 who has received a downscreen from 4. When 1 receives, 4 posts low and 3 continues to the strongside corner as another option.*

(14B)

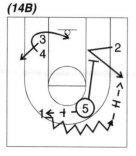

(16B)

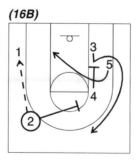

16B. *On the pass to 1, 3 screens 5 in the lane. 4 and 2 set staggered screens for 3.*

Side Out-of-Bounds Plays

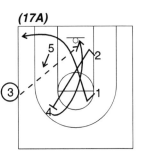

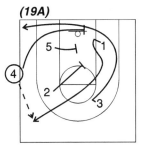

17A. Last-second special lob play: 5 sets up on the strongside block and asks for the ball. 3 inbounds (if he is a good passer), 4 is on the strongside high post, 1 on the weakside high post and 2 is above the weakside block.

17B. 1 cuts first and goes diagonally off 5 to the nearside corner. As 1 passes him, 2 comes up and sets a diagonal backscreen on 4 who, after faking to the ball, has stepped out. He goes over the top of 2 for a lob pass from 3. 5, 1 and 2 are the options if we have no lob pass.

18A. Misdirection successive double picks for shooters: 4 and 5 vertically screen down as 2 inbounds to 1 coming up to the ball after receiving a screen from 4. 1 dribbles to the weakside wing as 4 and 5 continue down and set baseline screens for 3. 1 passes to 3.

18B. 3 has the ball; 4 and 5 continue and set a double screen for 2 who can cut baseline to the low post or high off a screen from 1 as 4 curls around 5.

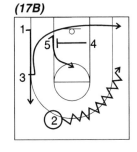

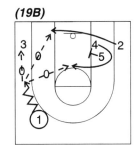

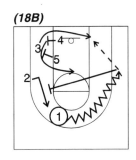

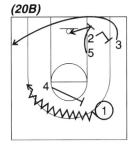

19A. Double screen for the shooter: 4 inbounds to 1 who receives a diagonal screen from 2 and a horizontal screen from 5. When 1 receives, 4 and 5 screen across the lane for 3 who breaks to the low post and then the corner looking for the ball.

19B. When 3 receives in the corner from 1, 4 circles into the lane around picks by 2 and 5. 2 steps out and comes to the ball for a scoring opportunity.

20. Zipper special on shooter being overplayed: 3 inbounds and 5 takes two steps down and screens for 1 breaking at the same time, 2 fakes up on the weak side and instead cuts across the lane for a surprise pass on the block from 3.

Option: Pass to 1, 4 screens for him in the two-man game as 5 and 2 set a staggered baseline screen for 3. If 1 passes back to 4, 2 is open on the wing.

Side Out-of-Bounds Plays

21A. In this play, 3 inbounds the ball; 4 and 5 are on the strong and weak-side blocks while 1 and 2 are on the strong and weak-side elbows. 1 screens away for 2 and, at the same time, 5 comes high to backpick 1's defender. 1 then circles 5 and continues around the baseline and uses a screen from 4 on the strongside block. 3 inbounds the ball to 2 and screens down for 1.

21B. 2 has the ball and may pass to 1 in the corner or use a backpick by 5 in the two-man game to dribble the ball to the other side of the court to 3 who has continued across after picking for 1.

22A. Special from a tight box set: 1 and 2 are low and 4 and 5 are set up high. First 1 backpicks 4 who looks for the lob pass from 3 inbounding the ball. Then 5 diagonally downscreens for 2 who pops out after 5 has screened for him.

22B. Option: On a pass to 1 instead of 4, 3 steps in and spots for a three-point shot. 2 does the same and 4 and 5 both post low setting up four different passing options for 1.

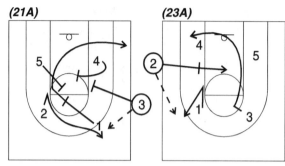

(21A)

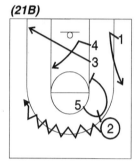

(21B)

(22A)

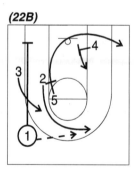

(22B)

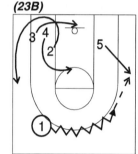

(23A)

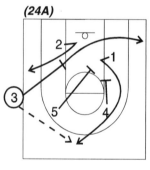

(24A)

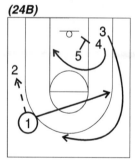

(24B)

23A. 2 inbounds to 1 stepping out and joins 4 in setting a double screen on the strongside baseline. Once 1 has received the pass, 2 cuts diagonally off the double screen looking for a pass from 1 as the first option.

23B. The second option is 1 reversing the ball back to 5 stepping out as 2 circles 4 and 3 and comes back into the lane. 3 and 1 interchange off of the ball on the weak side and 4 posts low or flashes to the ball if he is open.

24A. 3 inbounds to 1 who has come to the ball after receiving a double screen from 4 and 5. 3 then screens down for 2 on the strongside block. 2 pops out for a pass from 1 as 3 crosses the lane and clears to the other side.

24B. 2 has the ball and 1 interchanges with 3 as 5 screens 4 in the lane circling to the ball and the strongside low post. 2 can pass inside, penetrate, shoot or reverse the ball by passing to 3.

Under-the-Basket Plays

The philosophy of running under-the-basket or baseline out-of-bounds plays is consistent with our sideline objectives. Of primary concern is putting the ball in play with the intention of scoring or at least drawing a foul and going to the free-throw line.

Exerting extreme pressure on the defense and scoring quickly can demoralize opponents. Utilize all available screening techniques, and try to have your best shooters take the ball out and then step in and screen or be screened to get a good scoring opportunity. They also can decoy the defense to provide a teammate with a scoring opportunity.

Repeated practice against a live defense prepares players to handle all types of pressure. They must learn to recognize offensive rebounding opportunities as well as maintain proper defensive balance to be in position to stop the opposition's fast-break or transition game.

In all live full- and half-court drills, use the shot and game clocks to simulate actual conditions. Using the clocks in drills without defense perfects timing and shows the players how much time is required to run each play and its various options.

Special Situation Plays

We also have out-of-bounds plays to deal with every (we think) conceivable out-of-bounds situation from many different areas of the court and point differentials. We constantly refine them and provide players with options that help them react to different defensive and pressure situations.

Again, utilize the clocks in all of these situations and try to anticipate anything that might arise in regulation and/or overtime. *YOU MUST PREPARE FOR PRESSURE BEFORE YOU HAVE TO CONFRONT IT.*

Coach's Edge

Every out-of-bounds play is important, and it's critical that the coach and players know how many time-outs remain and the rules governing who may call or signal for a time-out. International rules are quite different from American rules. An inadvertent call can be the difference between winning and losing.

Baseline Out-of-Bounds Plays

1A. *4 inbounds the ball and looks first for 3 cutting off of a back screen from 2. Our second option is to 2 cutting to the ball side corner off of a back screen in the lane from 5 who then pivots to the ball. 4 looks to pass to 2 and then he cuts away from the ball.*

(1A)

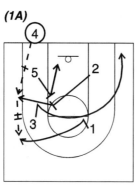

(3A)

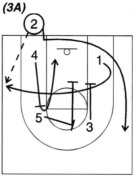

3A. *2 inbounds, 4 backpicks up for 5 who cuts down the lane at the same time 3 screens down for 1 who uses the screen set by 3 and a screen set by 5 to come the ball-side corner for the pass from 2 as 4 posts low.*

1B. *3 now sets a screen for 4 on the weakside baseline. 5 is posted low as an option for 2 if he has no shot and 1 is above the ballside elbow as an outlet and also to receive a pass and reverse the ball to 4 looking for the ball after hesitating and using the screen from 3.*

(1B)

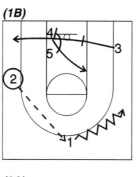

(3B)

3B. *1 has the ball in the corner for a shot, a pass to 5 inside or looks for 2, the inbounds passer who has cut away from the ball and used a backscreen from 3 to circle to the ball at the top of the circle where receives another screen from 4.*

2A. *3 inbounds with 4 and 5 on the blocks and 1 and 2 each lined up almost directly behind the post men. 2 screens down and inside 4 and reverse pivots into the lane for the lob from 3 as 2 steps to the corner. As 4 curls, 1 fakes and cuts to the weakside corner off of 5 looking for a pass, especially if the defense shades 4 inside.*

(2A)

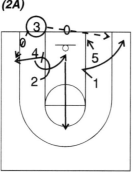

(4A)

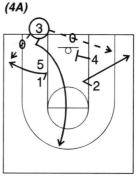

4A. *Return pass to the inbounder (3) which sets up a screen-and-roll situation for 3 when 4 sets a diagonal back screen for him once he has received the pass from 1. 5 posts low and 2 fakes in and spots up in the corner.*

2B. *If these options are not open, we pass to 2, and 3 steps inside and posts up after faking the cutaway (buttonhook).*

(2B)

(4B)

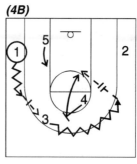

4B. *On the pass to 1 in the corner, 3 has cut directly up the lane where he turns and faces, and looks for a pass and possibly a shot. 4 sets a screen for him and 3 can penetrate and drive to the goal, look for 4 on the roll or pitch to 2 in the corner for a shot.*

Baseline Out-of-Bounds Plays

Coach's Edge

It's important to remember that in our diagrammed out-of-bounds plays we are flexible and have no problem changing the position of any of our players. We can run any play for any player. We work very hard in practice having different players inbound the ball.

5A. *Unbalanced stack with 5 and 3 on the ballside block and 2 and 4 on the weakside elbow:* As 3 steps to the corner from behind 5, 2 sets a backpick for 4. 1 can pass to 3 in the corner, 5 on the block or 4 coming to the ball.

5B. *The rule for 1 is that he must cut opposite the pass. He can pass to 3, cut away and use a screen from 4 or he can cut straight up the lane to the top of the key to receive a pass from 3 to shoot, reverse the ball or open up the inside for 5.*

6A. *3 inbounds and 2 fakes a screen down on 4 and cuts horizontally to the strongside corner using a screen from 5. At the same time, 1 breaks to the wing as an outlet. The first option is the pass to 2 in the corner; the second option is for 3 to look inside for 4 coming off of 5's second screen inside.*

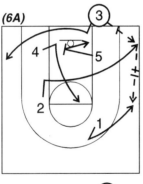

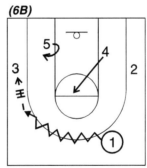

6B. *Our next option after the pass to 2 is 3 cutting away from the pass, using the third pick by 5 and coming to receive the ball after 2 passes to 1. 3 can shoot or pass inside to 5 if we have created a mismatch by causing the defense to switch.*

7A. *Unbalanced set: 3 inbounds and 5 points the ball on lane with 5 above the strongside elbow. 1 and 2 begin parallel to 4 and 5 but they are in the middle of the free-throw lane. 4 side-screens for 2 who breaks to the ball-side wing, then 4 continues down to screen for 1 breaking up to the top. The pass to 2 is Option 1.*

7B. *Option 2 is 4 posting low and 3 moving away from the ball and 2 passing to 5 inside or 1 at the top of the key who then can reverse the ball to 3 or dribble and look in to 4.*

Baseline Out-of-Bounds Plays

(8A)

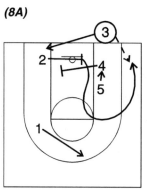

8A. *2 sets a horizontal backpick for 4 and then cuts over 5 to the ballside corner for the pass from 3 and 4 looks for the ball inside as the first or second option. 5 steps to the ball looking for a pass as well. 1 is back as an outlet in what we call center field.*

(10A)

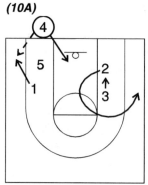

10A. *4 inbounds to 1 stepping to the ballside corner or to 3 after 2 has circled him and cut to the weakside wing. If 4 passes to 1, he hesitates one count and steps into the lane.*

(8B)

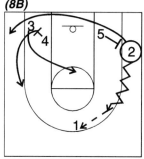

8B. *3 cuts away from the pass and we try to reverse the ball to him or look inside if his cutoff of the big men causes a switch by the defense.*

(10B)

10B. *When 1 receives in the corner, 5 reverse pivots and sets a screen for 1 and they run a pick and roll play and 1 also looks inside to make a pass to 4 or passes to 2 or 3 who posts inside.*

(9A)

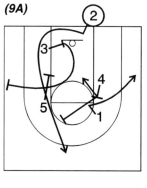

9A. *Triple screen for 2 who is our inbounds passer. 4 backpicks 1 to free him to receive the inbounds pass and then continues and joins 3 and 5 in setting a triple staggered screen for 2 who has hesitated after his pass to 1 and then circled around the screens to the ball.*

(11A)

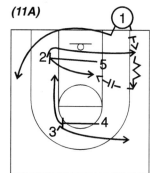

11A. *1 inbounds to 2 following 5 screening across the lane for him and at the same time 3 cuts off of a screen by 4. 2 has the ball and 5 reverse pivots and comes back to the ball.*

(9B)

9B. *1 looks to pass to 2 for the shot off of the screen, 3 circles back out around 5 who then steps to the low post on the ball side to provide an inside scoring option.*

(11B)

11B. *1 goes out away from the ball after his pass. If 5 isn't open and 2 decides to pass to 3, we have a chance to reverse the ball to 1 and look inside.*

Baseline Out-of-Bounds Plays

(12A)

12A. *3 inbounds to 2 who cuts off of a double screen set by 4 screening down and 5 on the block as 1 steps back as an outlet.*

(14A)

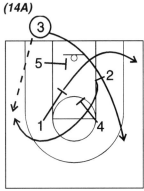

14A. *3 inbounds to 2 circling to the ball off of a triple pick set by 5, 1 and 4 in the lane area. If not free, 2 looks inside to 4 coming to the ball or to 1 in the far corner. 3 cuts opposite his inbounds pass.*

(12B)

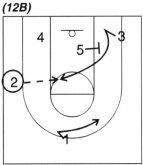

12B. *3 cuts away from the ball and will circle back off of another double by 4 and 5. 2 has a shot or a pass to 3 inside or 1 outside in a position to penetrate or bang the ball inside or to look for 2 coming to the ball.*

(14B)

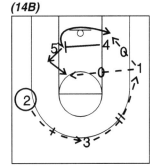

14B. *If 2 has exhausted his options he may pass to 3 who then has shooting options or the chance to reverse the ball to 1 who looks inside.*

(13A)

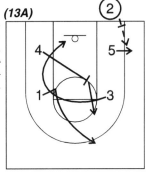

13A. *2 inbounds to 5 stepping to the corner or to 3 who cuts to the basket off of the backpick from 4 and 1 breaks out to be an outlet.*

(15A)

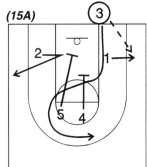

15A. *3 inbounds to 1 who has stepped to the corner while 4 and 5 cut to the baseline and set a double screen on 3's defender so 3 may cut up the lane for the ball. At the same time 2 must fake and pull his man to the wing.*

(13B)

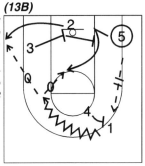

13B. *If 1 gets a pass from 5, 4 comes up and sets a pick for a two-man play with 1 as 2 cuts to the corner of the ball side off of a screen by 3 inside.*

(15B)

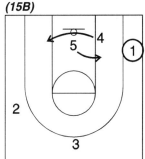

15B. *1 has the pass option to 3 and 3 may shoot or swing the ball to 2 for the shot or 2 looks inside for 4 who has circled around 5 and come back across the lane and to the ball.*

Baseline Out-of-Bounds Plays

16A. *3 inbounds and 4 screens down on 1 and at the same time 2 fakes in and steps out, permitting 5 to dive to the goal for a pass.*

(16A)

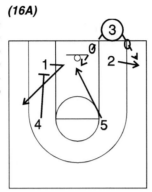

(18A)

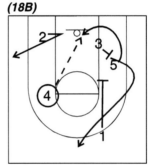

18A. *3 inbounds to 5 stepping to the corner and 1 pops to the sideline and 4 steps back to the top of the key. After the pass, 3 cuts hard up the lane. 5 hits 1 with a pass and 1 passes to 4. As 4 receives, 2 takes a step to the ball and makes a reverse pivot and looks for the lob pass from 4.*

16B. *If 5 is not free, 3 passes to 2 and he can cut away or up the middle off of 5. 4 posts low and 2 can pass to 3 who shoots or he can pass to 1.*

(16B)

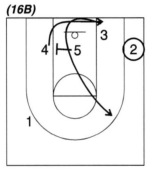

(18B)

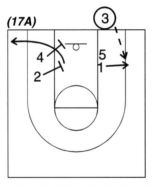

18B. *If not there, 3 and 4 use the pinch post.*

17. *3 inbounds to 1 stepping to the corner, to 5 stepping in or to 4. 2 picks down on 3 with 4 and after 3 circles them, 2 curls, too.*

(17A)

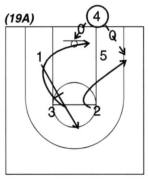

(19A)

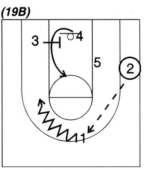

19. *4 inbounds to 2 in the corner after 5's backpick. 1 then backpicks 3 for the lob from 2 or 2 hits 1 and 1 looks for 5 or for 4 coming off of 3 inside.*

(17B)

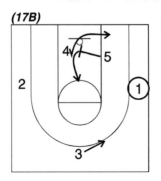

(19B)

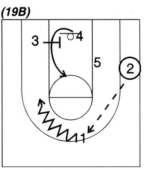

Baseline Out-of-Bounds Plays

(20A)

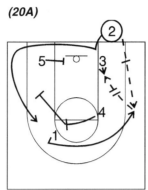

20A. As 2 takes the ball out, 1 uses a screen by 4 to get free and to receive the ball. After passing, 2 cuts away off of a screen by 5 and 4 and then he steps out as 1 looks for 3 on the low post.

(22A)

22A. 3 inbounds the ball to 2 as 2 cuts off of a double screen set by 4 and 5. 1 steps out to the weakside wing as 4 cuts to the block after his pick for 2. 5 steps up and across the lane looking to set a screen on 1's defender.

20B. If this pass isn't there, 1 can pass to 4 who reverses the ball to 3 who can shoot or look inside as 4 picks away.

(20B)

(22B)

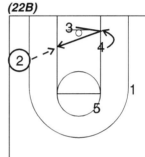

22B. This action frees 3 to fake away and look for a pass from 2. If this is not available we look to reverse the basketball.

(21A)

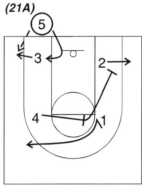

21A. 5 inbounds to 3 stepping out and then steps in for a quick return pass. 4 horizontally picks away for 1. 5 can pass to 3 or if 3 is fronted, 5 hits 1 and he passes inside to 3.

(23A)

23A. 3 inbounds, 1 sets a backpick for 2 who spins and goes around a two man screen on the strong side set by 4 and 5 and 1 pivots and looks for 3 as he cuts away after passing the ball to 2.

21B. If this is not open, 1 can look for 2 off a screen by 4 on the weak side and then 4 posts up.

(21B)

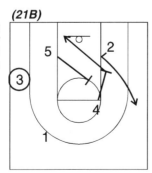

(23B)

23B. If 2 has no shot he swings the ball to 5 stepping out and we again reverse the ball and look inside. We like to have 4 and 5 screen each other diagonally.

Baseline Out-of-Bounds Plays

24. *3 inbounds and this is an example of the curl move from out of bounds. 3 passes to 1 shooting out to the wing and once the ball is passed 2 circles 5 on the baseline. 1 passes to 4 and he looks inside to 2 if free or he fakes to him and tries to pass to 5 who has posted up to the ball.*

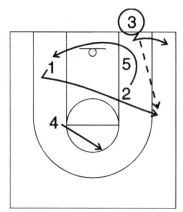 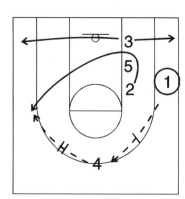

Coach's Edge

It's important to realize that if our first option is not open we are not done with our play. Most defenses gear themselves to stop the first option and they are not really prepared to stop a planned secondary thrust.

Full-Court Out-of-Bounds Play

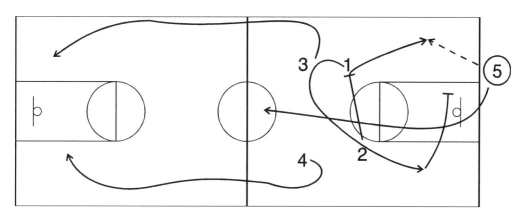

Out-of-Bounds Play Following a Violation or a Time-Out

5, or one of our better passers, inbounds the basketball. His first option is to look for one of our players going long, especially if the defense tries to come up and pressure. If the 4 or 5 positions are not free, 2 and 1 pick across and move to the ball. The man farthest from the ball screens first. He then pivots back to the ball. Both 1 and 2 must continually work to get free. If 1 receives, 2 sets a screen on the inbounds passer's man and if 2 receives, 1 picks 5's man. We then try to go full court to make the defense pay for trying to press us. 5, or whoever inbounds, has the responsibility of posting up in the middle as the press breaker.

Three-Quarters Court Out-of-Bounds Play

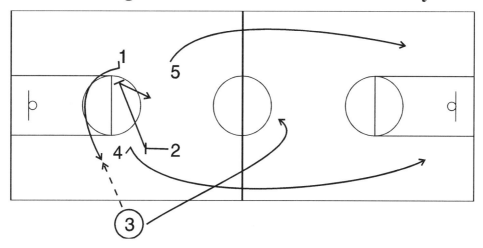

Sideline Out-of-Bounds Play

3 inbounds as 5 fakes to the ball and then goes long. At the same time, 2 screens down on 4 and then across for 1. 4 breaks long and 3 again looks for the long pass first. His next options are to 1 using 2's pick or to 2 pivoting back to the ball. The inbounder, 3, cuts to the middle as a press breaker or to run directly to the basket on the fast break. We automatically run our transition offense if the break is not there.

We always look to advance the ball upcourt as quickly as possible using the long pass.

** Any of our players can be placed in any position when we run these plays. The object is to score and it's the coach's responsibility to best utilize his personnel effectively.

9
Executing the Offense

When you have two wings crossing along the baseline or even at the elbow areas with a single or a double post, it's sound offensive theory to have one man cross under both posts and the other man cut over one and under the other. This simple offensive maneuver — varying our cuts — forces the defense to make constant adjustments and play us honest. They never know what our offense is going to do in a given situation or on a specific play.

Some coaches also designate the player on the ball side as the screener on crosses while others permit the player calling his teammate's name as the designated screener or picker. This is a valuable aid in teaching players how to read and attack defenses.

We work hard and drill on how we want attack the defenses our opponent's use against the single and double stack. Do they follow or go over the top on the single, slide through one man removed, switch or body check?

On the double, do they switch on the baseline, play it straight, invert and switch, follow and fight through, bump or body check? We have plays to counter each situation, and we work continuously to take advantage of the weaknesses in each defensive option, constantly probing for opportunity or high-percentage shots and mismatch opportunities.

Every time a team double-teams or traps, we try to make them pay by hitting the **OPEN MAN**. We try to pass the ball before the trap forms, and our players know that a man is always free when the defense double-teams or traps. We want these open men to rotate and cut to open areas of the court so that they can take advantage of the defense's weaknesses.

We want our players to learn how to turn and face, and protect the ball. Displaying confidence and not losing our composure are very effective methods which we use to pick apart defenses. Finding the open man will make the defense pay the price for its gambles. Our principle of in, out and over is paramount when attacking our opponent.

Our players are taught that closing the distance between them and their defender is a means of getting free and enables them to more easily receive a pass or make a cut. Moving behind the screener when cutting without the ball is more difficult to defend and presents us with more offensive options. If we feel our players have mastered the technique of reading the defense, we relax this rule.

We try to develop thinking players. Each play we run on offense sets up an option for our next play and is designed to make the defense more wary of the other situations we will force them to defend. There is a natural progression to what plays and options we are trying to run, and once we realize something is successful, we continue to take advantage of it. We believe in the axiom that you don't change something if it's effective.

Our offensive philosophy is designed to make the opponent's best players defend. We run plays at them designed to make them play defense, especially if they are scoring a great deal or if they are in foul trouble. One way to stop offensive threats is to break their concentration and rhythm. Forcing them to play defense takes their minds off of what they might think is their primary responsibility.

We switch the Box Offense into the 1-4 High or the 1-4 Low for specific reasons. In the case of the 1-4 High, we are able to immediately open up the floor against an aggressive and pressuring opponent to run some backdoor, lob plays or clearouts. In our 1-4 Low, we give our point man the entire frontcourt to isolate his defender forcing trapping or double-teaming defenses to come a long way to try and get the ball. Both sets are extremely effective in a close game when the score is tied or we are ahead with not much time left.

We also use these options to change the game's tempo. Passing the basketball has become a lost art and turnovers are surely the bane to a coach's existence. We try to find ways to make players become better passers. In our drills, instead of the coach, assistant coach or manager making the passes to shooters or initiating a breakdown situation, players perform this function. This not only improves their skill level, but makes them more aware of the importance of successfully delivering the basketball. We emphasize that even a great shooter can't score if the pass to him is ineffective and use the name of an outstanding modern player to get this point across.

Coach's Edge

When designing offensive plays, limit the defense's opportunities to double-team and trap, and also provide your players with the options and the confidence needed to take advantage of weaknesses in gambling defensive tactics. When opponents gamble, it shows how much they fear your offensive movement and ability. Repeatedly emphasize this to your players.

Coach's Edge

Individual players master certain techniques and become specialists in these areas. Encourage your players to teach these specialties to teammates. Players tend to listen to and respect greatness and ability in other players. Many times they are more willing to accept constructive assistance from each other, especially if the coach gives them time to work together.

Coaches should force the defense to stop every possible offensive tactic when preparing to play against their teams. Opponents should not only have to worry about defending your half-court sets, but also your full-court transition game, fast-breaking tactics, motion offense, all types of out-of-bounds scoring plays, aggressive rebounding tactics and multiple offensive moves.

Every good defensive coach prepares his team to stop the offensive moves and tendencies of each opponent. We want our opponents to concern themselves with an offense that not only takes what the defense gives it by teaching our players to read their defenders, but we also want the opposition to devote valuable practice time worrying about an offense that is unpredictable, multiple and fundamentally sound. We want them to have to prepare to defend each of the following situations:

1. Dribble penetration and drives to the basket.
2. The penetrate and pitch or draw and kick option.
3. The three-point shot.
4. The screen-and-roll and all of its options.
5. Multiple screens (single, double and triple), and staggered or unified blocks.
6. Vertical, horizontal, diagonal and sidescreens.
7. Backpicks and downscreens.
8. Curls or loops, flares and slashes.
9. Cross-the-lane and comeback screens.
10. Pick-the-picker tactics.
11. Shuffle and weakside cuts.
12. The lob or alley-oop pass.
13. Backdoor cuts.
14. Splitting the post or scissoring.

15. The pinch post option.

16. The handback and inside handoff.

17. Isolations or clearouts.

18. Misdirection movement.

19. High-Low action.

20. Buttonhooks.

21. Mismatches and post-ups.

22. Weaving action and crossing with and without the ball designed to split the defense.

Summary of Drilling Emphasis

In our breakdown drills for teaching offense, we try to follow a standardized procedure and method. We don't presume it to be an end-all for coaches, but it may serve as a guide and encourage you to dissect and study your present system. If it whet's your appetite and challenges you to evaluate your present methods, this book will have served its purpose.

After we introduce and explain a drill to our players, we begin by practicing each drill without defense. This helps our players learn the necessity of proper spacing and timing, and the important role faking plays in optimum offensive execution. We walk through each drill, asking the players to visualize every move they make as if they were competing against a live defense. We then practice each movement at full speed without the defense, correcting our players as we progress.

After they have satisfactorily grasped the concepts, we add live defense in 2-on-2, 3-on-3 and 4-on-4 drill situations in the frontcourt. Our players rotate clockwise from offense to defense, playing each offensive spot and defending from each position on the floor.

We emphasize:

- Faking without the ball to establish position.
- Ball fakes which force players to read the defense.
- Movement, and changing speed and direction.
- Being late rather than early when cutting off of screens.
- Establishing eye contact with the player with the ball.
- Creating proper angles to develop our passing techniques.
- Screening your own defender.
- Splitting the defenders on switches.
- Pick the picker and/or your own defender.

- Cutting, screening or spotting-up once they have passed the ball.
- Establishing the triple threat position when we receive the ball.
- Downscreens and backpicks.
- Cutting behind screens rather than going over the top until players are reading the defense.
- Timing, spacing and execution.
- Offensiverebounding.
- Every offensive player must always see the ball!!

Our rule is that we complete each drill successfully by playing until the offense makes a basket or the defense recovers the basketball. We alternate and use each side of the floor because in the offense, we enter our plays on either side of the court.

Normally our big men only play the high or low post positions, but we may permit them to play the point to make them understand the importance of providing a good passing angle for the passer when you don't have the ball. Both receiver and passer must work at creating proper passing lanes and must hit the open man on offense.

Emphasize the following:

- Reading the defense
- Passing options
- Meeting the pass
- Faking without the ball
- Establishing eye contact among the offensive players
- Proper passing angles and technique
- Successfullycompletingeachdrill
- Forcing the defense to constantly make decisions

Teaching method:

- Explain the drill
- First practice with no defense to familiarize players with the drill and for proper timing and spacing
- Graduate from 2-on-2 to 3-on-3 for options and movement
- Rotateplayersclockwisefromoffense to defense to help the players understand the differences in playing each position.
- Alternate and change sides of the court in drills

Specific Breakdown Drills for Teaching the Ballside Zipper Entry

(1)

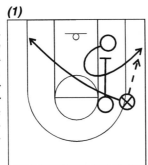

1. Downscreen from the high post to receive the ball in the corner: *Wait and cut over or under the screen. After the pass, the passer moves and/or cuts to an open area dictated by his defender's action.*

(3)

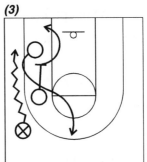

3. Downscreen and slash to the top of the key: *The greater the distance the defense must cover, the more difficult the defensive task.*

(2)

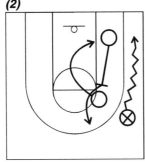

2. Backpick and step out: *Man receiving the screen cuts inside or outside depending on how his defender plays him.*

(4)

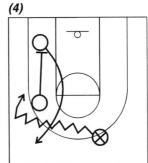

4. Downscreen and circle to the top of the key: *Wait for the screen to be set. It's more difficult for the defender to cover a cut from a standstill position.*

(5)

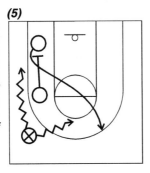

5. Downscreen and diagonal cut over or under to the top of the key: *The passer has two passing options and must establish the proper passing angles with the help of the receivers.*

(7)

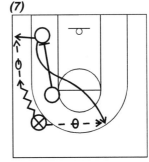

7. Downscreen and curl diagonally up and across after the screen: *Screener posts or steps out to the corner to open the floor or go one-on-one with the ball.*

(6)

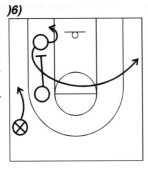

6. Downscreen and/or circle clearout for man setting the screen who is now the low post player: *He may also step to the corner after the low man clears.*

(8)

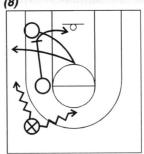

8. Downscreen, wait and circle to turn out to the corner: *Circle move is to the strongside corner giving the passer two options — corner and/or low post.*

Specific Breakdown Drills for Teaching
Weakside Zipper Moves

(1)

1. Backscreen and step out: *Cutter waits until the screen is set before moving. This will set up the lob pass or stepout by the screener for the shot.*

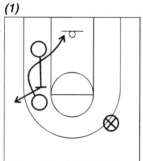

(3)

3. Upblock, fake flare and cut inside: *Used when the defense is anticipating a flare cut after a blind backscreen.*

(2)

2. Upblock and flare or fade: *Low man screens high and the man waiting for the screen fakes to get the defender to help towards the middle of the lane.*

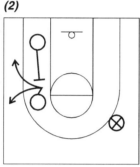

(4)

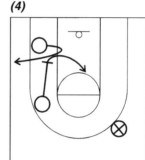

4. Downscreen, wait and pop to the corner or to the wing: *We want the man receiving a pick to vary his cuts to keep the defense honest.*

(5)

5. Downscreen and cut inside and out: *The player must wait for the screen before he moves.*

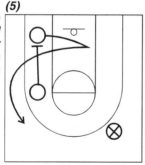

(7)

7. Downscreen and step out and then over: *Move the defense in different directions; vary the speed of your cuts and fakes.*

(6)

6. Downscreen and circle over, across, and under or over: *Vary your cuts.*

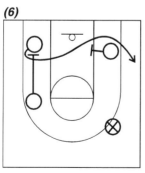

(8)

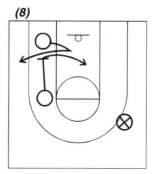

8. Downscreen and fade: *Good move to set up the skip pass.*

Breakdown Drills

These are some of the drills we use throughout the season to work on and perfect our offensive execution. **It's important to try to alternate sides with each drill.**

(4)

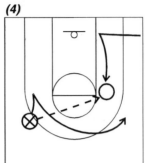

4. Pass, pinch post and handback: Entry pass to the pinch post man (outside of the elbow) "V" fake and cut outside the post and receive a handback. This drill begins our preparation for pinch post continuity.

1. Pass and bury: Point man passes to the wing who has popped out from the strongside low post position or from the strongside elbow.

(1)

(5)

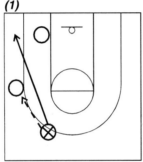

5. Pass, pinch post and follow to wing: Passer fakes handback and cuts to wing. Be may cut over or under the post player depending on simulated or live defense. This can set up such options as the screen-and-roll, one-on-one and/or shuffle cut moves.

2. Pass and diagonally screen away: Pass to wing and diagonally screen away for the weakside post man who waits for the screen and "V" fakes in before coming to the ball.

(2)

(6)

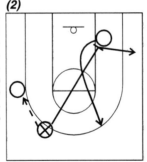

6. Pass, fake and screen the point off the ball: Most effective when post player has the ability to penetrate off the dribble. We use it in the box offense for our wings and power forwards.

3. Pass, screen away and step back to the ball: Point passes to the wing and screens away for the weakside elbow. Following the cut by the man on the elbow, the point steps back to the ball.

(3)

(7)

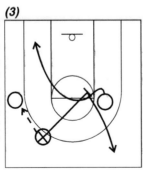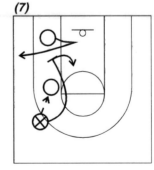

7. Pass and vertically screen for a shooter in the low post: The point passes to strongside post, then cuts inside or outside of the ball to set a screen on the block for the shooter who waits, fakes and moves to an area for a pass and shooting opportunity.

Breakdown Drills

1. Dribble entry, post pass and pindown for the shooter in the low post area: On the pindown, the low post player has options to pop out, fade, step in and screen.

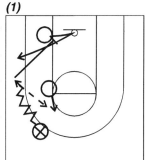

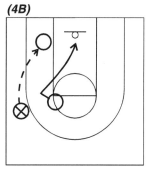

4B. Pass to the low post by the point, and the high post cuts to execute the give-and-go.

2. Entry pass, diagonal low post screen and stepout after low post curl.

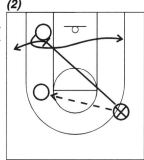

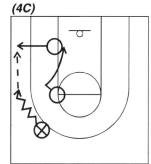

4C. Pass to the pivot stepping out and the high post executes a give-and-go cut.

3. Dribble entry, high post pass and give-and-go: On this move, it's important to emphasize the value of the fake, change of speed and direction by the cutter, and ball fakes by the passer!

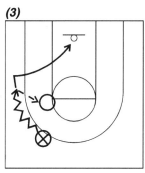

5. UCLA pass to the wing and the point almost horizontally screens the high post and then steps out: We encourage the high post player to fake to the ball and cut behind his defender. This may free him, but it also helps the low post player.

4A. Pass-and-cut: The wing passes to the low post, fakes and cuts to the basket. An example of the give-and-go.

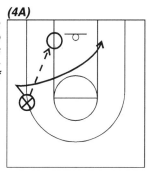

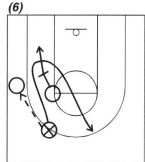

6. UCLA pass, cut, stop, receive a return screen and screen again: A change of direction and speed by the cutter to free himself or his teammate cannot be overemphasized.

Breakdown Drills

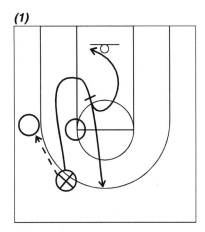

(1)

1. UCLA wing pass entry, vertical cut and return to backscreen: *This is a good option when the pass to the high post is overplayed and when your opponents chase the backpicker.*

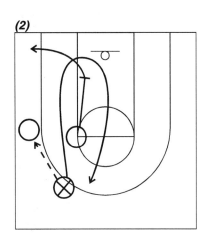

(2)

2. UCLA wing pass entry, vertical cut and stop to wait for downscreen from post: *When executed properly, this can cause indecision on the part of both the point and post defenders.*

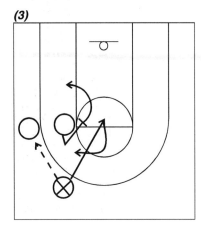

(3)

3. UCLA wing pass entry, vertical cut away and stop: *We then come back to the ball without waiting for a screen. We instead create a brush block with a change of speed and direction.*

Two things to remember:

- First practice without a defense, then include the defenders as you build two-, three-, four- and five-man sequences.
- If a player doesn't receive a return pass after he makes a pass and cut, he should always screen another teammate or find a teammate who can screen for him.

Additional Multiple Player Drills for Building the Box Offense

Screen-and-Roll Drills for 3 and 4 Players

Three separate player lines off the court alongside the spots or positions you are using.

1. Point-to-wing entry: *Low post backpick for the point man and then an elbow wing screen-and-roll. Emphasize timing, spacing and three players working together.*

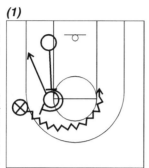

2. UCLA point-to-wing entry and wing and post screen-and-roll: *Post picks the point, steps out and goes to screen for the wing with the ball. The wing then dribbles over the screen to penetrate the middle.*

3. *Post player flashes to set a screen on the wing after the strongside post man sets a slash screen away for him, screening away and then back to the ball to move the defense in two directions on the same play.*

4. Weakside side or backscreen and flash screen to the point of the ball: *Player reverse pivots and goes over the top on the first screen.*

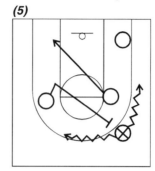

5. Blind screening angle from the weakside high post: *Interchanging the post players without screening.*

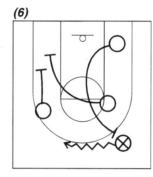

6. Screen from the low post to the wing at the same time as a double staggered screen away: *The synchronization and timing of offensive movements is the key to success.*

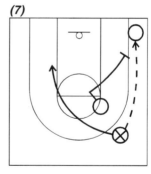

7. *Pass and cut away and then the elbow to the corner screen-and-roll.*

**** *We are trying to emphasize the advantages of setting two-man play screens from different angles on the court.*

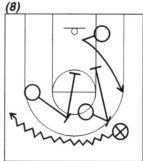

8. Double staggered high post screen-and-roll and then a double staggered screen for a shooter: *This is an example of individual players setting more than one screen on the same play.*

Specific Box Offense Maneuvers from a Five-Man Set

(1A)

1A. Isolation for the point man: As 1 penetrates off the screen by 5, 2 clears out across the lane to set up a screen-and-roll or isolation for 1.

(1C)

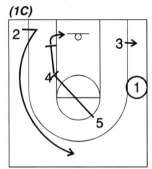

1C. 3 continues to the strongside corner and 4 and 5 set a staggered double screen for 2 coming high from the baseline.

(1B)

1B. Curl, loop or circle: 1 has the ball on the wing: 5 steps back and 4 screens down on 3 who circles into the lane for a pass from 1.

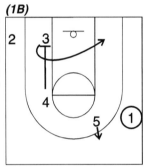

(1D)

1D. If 1 passes to 3 in the near corner, 4 comes and posts across the lane, 5 gains his position on the weakside board and 2 covers back defensively.

(1E)

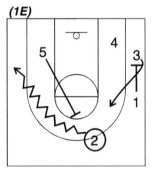

1E. If 1 elects to pass to 2 at the top of the key, 2 can shoot or run a high screen-and-roll or the pinch post option with 5.

We constantly emphasize the following points in our drills and practice preparation:

- Penetration
- Defensivebalance
- Offensive rebounding
- Timing

- Spacing
- Player movement without the ball
- Reversing the ball
- Reading the defense

Specific Box Offense Maneuvers from a Five-Man Set
Optional curl setup

(2A)

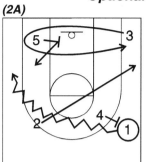

(2B)

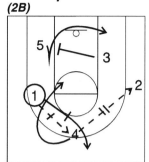

2A. *4 and 1 screen and roll from the wing to the middle as 2 clears across the lane to the weak side vacating the area as 3 curls around 5. This also permits 1 to dribble to the other side of the court to isolate 5 on the low post. We often use this maneuver with our small men causing the defense to switch creating mismatches in our favor and indecision by the defense.*

2B. *If 1 cannot pass to 5 he can pass to 4 who will then reverse the ball back to 2 on the opposite wing. We have now changed sides and reversed the ball to move the defense.*

Curl or loop with dribble entry by point to the wing

(3A)

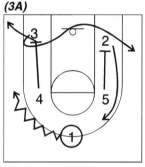

(3C)

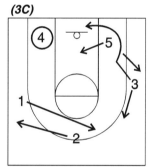

3A. *1 dribbles to the wing and looks to penetrate as 4 vertically screens down on 3. 4 pops to the corner and 5 vertically screens down on 2 as the ball reaches the wing.*

3C. *4 can go one-on-one, pass to 5 flashing across the low post or to 2 after he receives a screen from 1.*

(3B)

(3D)

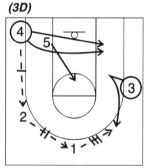

3B. *1 has the option to penetrate to the basket, pass to 4 in the near corner or to 2 at the top of the key. If 4 receives, he can look to go one-on-one.*

3D. *Another option if 4 has the ball in the corner is to have him pass to 2 and we can reverse the ball to 1 and then 3 as 4 executes a baseline flex cut off of 5. 5 then flashes into the lane looking to score.*

Specific Box Offense Maneuvers from a Five-Man Set

1A. Five-man screen-and-roll drills from the area of the high post: 5 sets a screen for 1 and when 1 passes him with the dribble he rolls to the basket. As the screen is set, 3 clears across the lane and rubs off of 2 to the corner. 1 may penetrate as well.

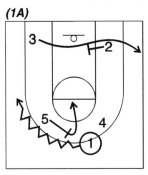
(1A)

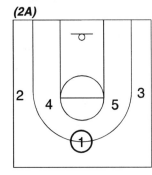
(2A)

We emphasize:
• A triple threat stance with the ball.
• Each player is positioned to best take advantage of his individual abilities.

2A. 1-4 High diagonal backscreen series: The 1-4 high is a set we use against pressure defense.

1B. 5 sets the screen and he steps back. After 3 again clears to the weak side, 2 sets a backpick for 4 who looks for a lob pass from 1.

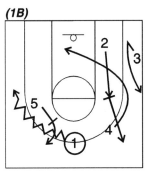
(1B)

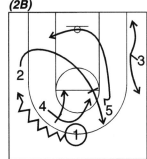
(2B)

2B. 1-4 high screen-and-roll with the wing clearing out and returning to set a weakside diagonal backscreen for 5 diving to the low post. Our first option is the screen-and-roll or clearout. The second option is to 5 on the low post.

1C. 1 may also pass to 4 on the low as 5 moves away to screen for 2 and then for 3.

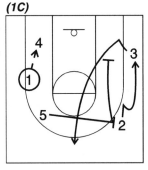
(1C)

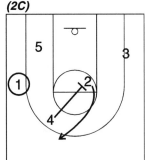
(2C)

2C. 2 receives a downscreen from 4 in the pick-the-picker option and 2 then steps out for a pass and shot as 3 fades to the corner. 4 can go and screen 3 or go to the low block.

1D. Option: 1 may elect to pass back to 5 before the screen for 2 is set and we look in (high-low) for 4 or reverse the ball to 3 so he can penetrate or shoot.

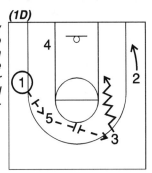
(1D)

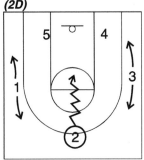
(2D)

2D. The options for 2 are to shoot, penetrate, pass or screen away.

Specific Box Offense Maneuvers from a Five-Man Set

2E. 1-4 High diagonal backscreen series (continued): If 1 elects to pass back to 4 on the pick-and-roll at the high post, 4 can penetrate, shoot, pass inside or reverse the ball.

(2E)

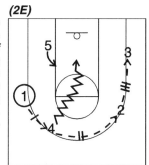

(2F)

2F. If 4 reverses to 2 and 2 passes to 3, 5 can set a misdirection backscreen from the weak side for 4. The use of ball reversal and misdirection keeps the defense occupied and we have more offensive flexibility in which to create and improvise.

Normal box set diagonal backscreen series

(3A)

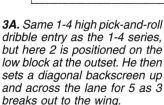

(3B)

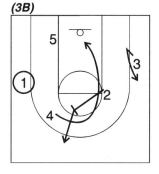

(3C)

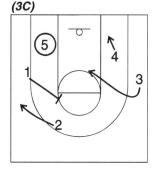

3A. Same 1-4 high pick-and-roll dribble entry as the 1-4 series, but here 2 is positioned on the low block at the outset. He then sets a diagonal backscreen up and across the lane for 5 as 3 breaks out to the wing.

3B. In the previous diagram the primary option was to 5 down low. Here, our second option is 2 setting a backscreen for 4 to set up a lob possibility and then stepping out for a shot opportunity. 1 may still pass to 5 in this situation.

3C. On the pass to 5 in the low post we have screening off the ball between 1 and 2 and a weakside cut option for 3 should the defenders turn their heads.

The Staggered Box Set: Five-Man Plays for Drilling Purposes

1. Special situation or need play with options: *High-low posts to take away the help.*

(1)

(4)

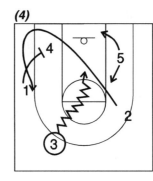

4. *1 now passes to 3 stepping out after he sets the pick and 2 cuts to the strongside corner opening the court for 3 to penetrate.*

*** The defense must follow 2 and honor his shooting ability. They cannot help on 3.*

2. Posting 4 low after the 5-1 high post screen-and-roll entry: *4 first fakes a screen away in the lane and then buttonhooks or reverse pivots back for the pass from the wing area.*

(2)

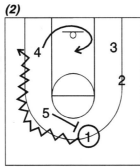

(5)

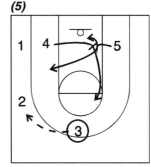

5. *When 3 receives at the top of the key he may pass back to 2 who may have interchanged with 1. As this occurs, 4 screens away for 5 in the low post area.*

3. *With the ball on the wing, 3 sets a diagonal backscreen from the weak to the strong side for 5 who goes behind the screen and looks for the lob pass or he turns and posts in the lane.*

(3)

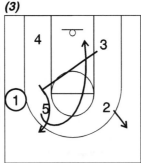

(6)

6. *We have time to reverse the ball again, as you normally do with a 30- or 35-second shot clock. We have time for 4 to break to the post area from the weak side and run a pinch post backdoor for 3.*

Different Sets for Building the Box Offense

- Position versatility and flexibility permit us to place added pressure on our opponent's individual defenders.

4. This option shows how we can also place 2 and 3 in the high post and 4 and 5 in the normally more comfortable low post positions that they occupy in a majority of offenses.

1. Basic set: Players may be in any of the spots or positions and we can begin our plays from either side of the court.

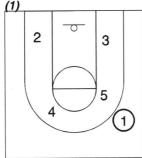

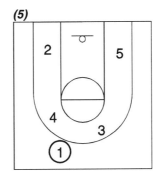

5. Here we have placed 2 and 3 and 4 and 5 in staggered high and low positions on opposite sides of the court.

2. Optional placement of 1, our point guard, versus pressure: Here he frees himself after the entry pass is made by screening another player and stepping out. He is setting a flare screen for 2.

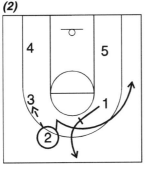

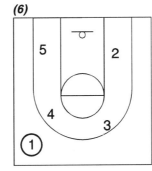

6. 4 and 5 are positioned on the same side of the lane to provide excellent high-low options and multiple screening options for our shooters.

3. Normal positions for the shooters are on the low post blocks. Here they are in excellent position to set and receive different types of screens.

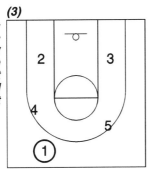

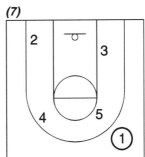

7. Our point guard can enter the ball from the middle of the court, above the elbows or from either wing position.

Different Alignments and Player Positioning

1. Normal or most frequently used set: 1, point; 2, shooting guard; 3, small forward; 4, power forward; 5, center.

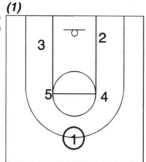

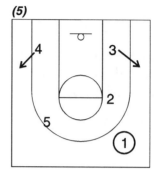

5. Staggered Set: 3 and 4 have fine opportunities to break out to the wings to receive the entry passes.

2. 1-4 High Set: Players may be shifted to any of four positions. The more versatile and skilled players could also play the 1 or point position. This is a good set to break pressure.

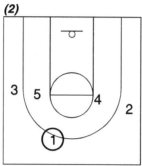

6. Unbalanced Set: Big and smaller players are placed diagonally opposite one another.

3. 1-4 Low Set: Brings the defenders to the baseline away from the ball, taking away the help and providing an opportunity for the point to create and penetrate.

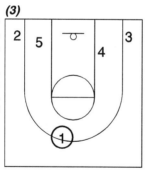

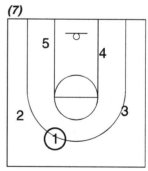

7. 1-2-2 Set: We open up the court from the outset. We can definitely place our post men in the wing or high post positions in this spread setup.

4. Double Stack Set: Facilitates crossing and double screen options, helps the wings or post men break out to receive the ball and provides many options for the point.

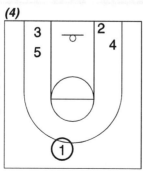

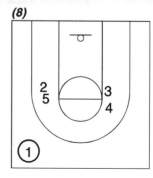

8. High Double Stack Alignment: This is popular on the college level as a delay or stall offense. It also provides more offensive options and flexibility.

Different Alignments and Player Positioning

(9)
(10)

9. Lopsided Setup:
The small men are outside of one free-throw lane and the big men outside the other. The key is that none of the positions or spots is parallel to one another which enhances our passing options.

10. Triple Post Set-up: *Same as the lopsided set. As Tex Winters describes the triple post, 1 theoretically can pass the ball to any of his teammates. We also give the man in the 3 position the option to begin in the corner or he can cut to this position once the play is signaled.*

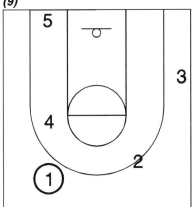

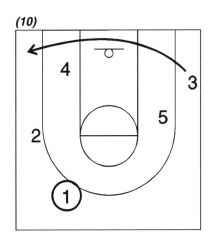

Spacing:

Initial spacing should be between 15 and 20 feet. This keeps the defense spread and maintains optimum passing lanes. The distance between the players will vary depending on the level of basketball your team plays.

Selected Plays for the Box Offense

Each play has a variety of options. Many screens are either normal frontscreens or backpicks which sometimes present more problems for the defense. Each play has options built in for the player the coach wants to do the shooting with alternatives to create opportunities for other players designed to counter any defensive scheme.

(1)

(4)

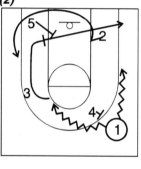

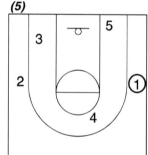

1. 4 sets a screen for 1 in the two-man game. 1 penetrates to the middle, 3 diagonally clears to the opposite wing area and 2 uses a baseline screen from 5 to clear out to the other side. After 1 uses his screen, 4 steps out or rolls to the basket, depending on how the defense reacts.

2. We now have an option run by 3 who, sets a staggered downscreen with 5 for 2 and then clears to the opposite corner leaving the post area for 5. All other options remain the same as in Diagram No. 1.

4. This is a variation with 2 backpicking 5 in the lane and 3 then screening for 2. The defense must decide how to play the small-to-big screen and they again must make a decision regarding how to defend the 3-to-2 pick. We also still have the two-man game option available.

5. Continuity if 1 is forced to the side-line.

(2)

(5)

(3A)

(6)

3A. Here is 1 with the ball after coming off the screen by 4 before he passes to 2.

6. These are his options if 1 penetrates to the middle but can't turn the corner.

3B. This shows the passing options available to 2. He has received the pass from 1 and 1 has cut away. In the previous diagram, instead of cutting away after the staggered screen, 3 curls around 5 and 2 comes to the top of the key on a diagonal cut instead of moving across the baseline.

(3B)

(7)

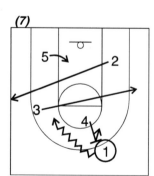

7. Same play but with a diagonal interchange between 2 and 3 without a screen a counter for equals switching.

**** *In each play or option we try to give the player with the ball the opportunity to pass to any of his teammates, emphasizing how important it is to establish open passing lanes.*

Selected Plays for the Box Offense

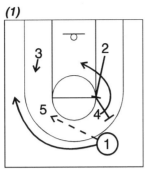
(1)

(5)

1. In the normal box set, we enter the ball to the high post and then run a variation of the pinch post or Adolph Rupp's Kentucky guard-around series. At the same time the entry pass is made, 2 on the weakside block backpicks 4 to set up a lob pass for a layup or dunk. 3 Takes a step up the lane to occupy the defense and 2 steps out to receive the ball.

2. 5 has the ball, passes it to 2 and 3 screens across for 4 and posts his man on the block looking for a pass from 2. If 3 doesn't receive the ball, he continues to the corner and 4 backpicks 5 and 5 then dives to the low post. 2 Has the option to penetrate, shoot, or pass to 3, 4 or 5. 1 must move his man to keep the defense occupied or to wait for a pass from 4.

3. This shows the options 2 has available to him once he has received the ball and the cuts in Diagram No. 2 have been made.

4. If 4 has the ball, 2 and 3 interchange and 4 and 1 can run a handoff and then two-man game option. 5 reads the ball to post up his defender or to cross the lane to the ball.

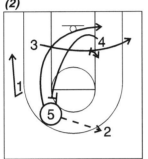
(2)

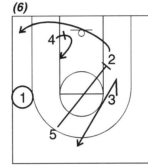
(6)

(3)
```
1        5
              3
   4
      2
```

(7)
```
2   4
          5
1
     3
```

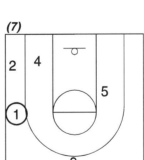

(4)

5. If 5 decides to pass to 1 in Diagram No. 1, 3 can screen 4 across the lane (or 4 can backpick 3) and then 2 down-screens 3 on the weak side (or 3 can backpick 2). 1 now has the option to pass inside to 4 on the block, reverse the ball to 5, beckon 5 to the ball for the two-man game, or penetrate and pitch.

6. The 2 man continues to the corner which establishes a 1-2-4 triangle or split post option and 5 screens down for 3 on the weak side so that we have continuity of movement, defensive balance and offensive rebounding position.

7. The positioning when 1 has the ball and our movement is complete. We are now in position to pass and cut or enter into our motion or free-lance game.

*****Again, we emphasize proper spacing, defensive balance, offensive rebounding position, ball movement with open passing lanes and multiple options for creating high-percentage shots and good scoring opportunities.

Selected Plays for the Box Offense
NBA option for the big man designed to take away defensive help

(1)

1. *4 sets a two-man game high entry screen for 1 who penetrates to the middle and kicks the ball back to 4 stepping out. When 4 receives the ball, 2 screens across the lane for 5. This is difficult to defend because it's small picking big. 3 then screens down on 2 in a pick-the-picker scheme. 4 has the option to pass inside to 5 or penetrate and/or pass to 2. On the original penetration, 1 always has the option to drive and create.*

(2)

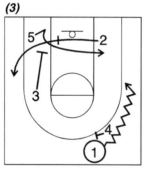

2. *4 has the ball. His options include having 1 and 3 set a double screen for 2.*

(3)

3. *Same play, but with the defense trying to force the point guard to the sideline. 4 can step back or screen diagonally away with 3. 2 also has the option to come high, stop and wait low, or cut back to the corner. His cut depends on how he thinks the defense will react.*

(4)

4. *2 has decided to come back to the ballside corner once he reads the defense and sees that 5 is unable to post up comfortably. If 1 has kept his dribble alive, we have many more options when he penetrates.*

(5)

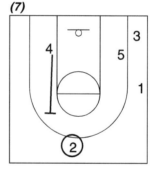

5. *1 has the ball and we are able to post 5 as 4 and 3 set a double screen away for 2, providing 1 with an additional option. The double screen may be staggered, but that depends on the position of the defense. If 5 is being fronted, we look to go high-low when 4 steps out after the screen in Diagram No. 3.*

(6)

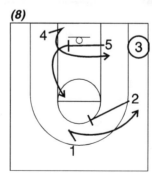

6. *This shows 4 stepping back for the high-low with 5, our posting action for 3 using a UCLA duck-in move, a possible 3-to-2 flash post and a backdoor or ball reversal to 2.*

(7)

7. *We have our positioning with 2 having received the ball off the double screen as 4 posts high outside the elbow and 3 continues to the corner to set up a triangle with 5 and 1. 2 and 4 also have the pinch post or two-man game option.*

(8)

8. *If 1 opts to pass to 3 in the near corner, we run our "big-man" screen across the lane, and 1 and 2 interchange and/or screen away to create outlet opportunities on the perimeter.*

**We always look to go inside and out and spot up for 3-point shots to counter double-teaming and teams trapping the low post.

Selected Plays for the Box Offense
High post screen-and-roll entry

1. *5 sets a high screen to help 1 penetrate as 2 simultaneously runs off of a brush block by 3. 3 then backpicks 4 for a lob pass or to establish low post position as 5 steps back or rolls depending on the defensive reaction. 3 waits as an outlet near the elbow area after he screens.*

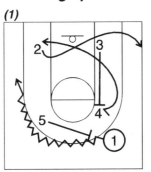

(1)

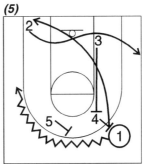

(5)

5. *We run the same play but enter with a staggered double high post screen-and-roll above or near the 3-point line. 2 runs off of 3, then 3 backpicks 4 in our pick-the-picker option.*

2. *The first option is an isolation opportunity for 1. Next, 5 steps back or rolls to the basket after his screen and the lob or low post pass to 4. If we don't have these options, we look for 3 coming off a screen by 5.*

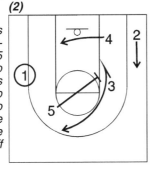

(2)

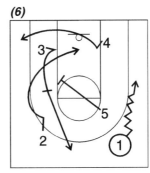

(6)

6. *Again, we run the same play but put our post men on the same side of the court. Instead of driving the middle, 1 changes direction and goes sideline which signals 4 to clear off of 3 who then backpicks 2 as 5 picks 3 in our pick-the-picker option.*

3. *Once 3 receives, he can shoot the 3-point shot or penetrate and drive to the goal. He also has the options to pitch to 2 or to post 5. He can pass back or pitch to 1. Once again we can post 4 or 4 can run an inside screen across the lane with 5.*

(3)

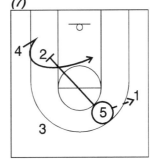

(7)

7. *Instead of screening as he did in Diagram No. 6, 5 steps back in position to reverse the ball to 3. Should he decide to return the ball to 1, he can set up 4 using a screen by 2 (small-on-big) to run a baseline flex cut to the ball or establish another two-man game with 1.*

4. *When 2 receives in the corner he can look to post 5. If 4 sees 5 fronted, he breaks diagonally to the ball or to the strong side elbow to set up the high-low for 5 inside while 3 and 1 pick away or interchange on the weak side.*

(4)

(8)

8. *With the ball in the hands of 1, 5 can screen diagonally away for 2 who can elect to come to the corner. Now 4 can come high or low off the second move by 5.*

Selected Plays for the Box Offense
Plays using curl, loop or circling action

1. Begin by having 5 pick for 1 in two-man game action. When this happens, 3 clears across the lane. After 3 has cleared, 4 vertically screens down 2's defender on the weakside block. 2 has moved up the lane to eliminate the 3 man switching to him, then circles into the lane around 4 and looks for a pass from 1. If the defense switches, 4 can step to the ball and create a mismatch.

2. After 5 screens 1, he can step back, roll to the basket or set a double staggered screen with 4 for 3 who comes from the weakside corner to the top of the key. 3 can also curl instead of cutting high off the screens by 4 and 5.

3. 2 has decided to flash to the corner instead of posting after he curls and 1 passes to him in the corner. 4 breaks to the strongside low post and looks for a pass from 2. 5 screens away for 3 on the weak side to take away the defensive help. He must look at the ball in case a trap or double-team develops inside.

4. 3 has the ball and 5 comes high to set a two-man game screen on the weak side as 1 and 2 interchange.

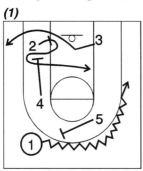
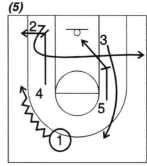
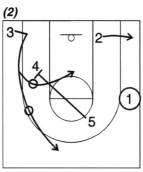
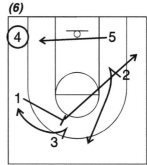
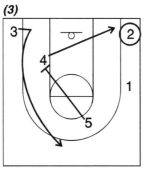
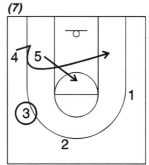

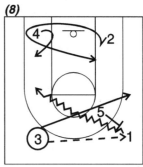

5. 1 dribbles to the sideline as 4 and 5 screen down on 2 and 3, respectively. 2 circles 4 and 3 uses the first screen by 5 to come up high. 4 then pops to the corner and 5 screens for 2.

6. 1 passes into the corner to 4 and interchanges on the outside with 3 and 2. 5 breaks across the lane looking for the pass from 4 if 4 isn't able to penetrate.

7. If 4 passes to 3 and we reverse the ball to 1 on the weak side, 5 screens for 4 and 4 runs a baseline flex cut to the ball. On a defensive switch or if the middle is open, 5 has the option to step into the lane for the ball.

8. Special play: 3 cuts to the corner to clear out the top of the key area after passing to 1 as 5 screens for 1. With 1 penetrating across in the two-man game, 2 circles off of 4 on the low post and clears out enabling us to isolate 4 inside. 5 and 3 screen for 2 on the weak side.

Selected Plays for the Box Offense
High post entry

1. *1 passes to one of the high post players, flares away against the pressure and uses a back-screen from the other high post man. The screener (4) steps out, giving 5 two options to reverse the ball. 2 fakes in, then steps out and, at the same time, 3 posts in the lane.*

2. *5 uses a skip pass to reverse the ball to 1 who can pass to 3 posting low. After either pass to 3 from 1 or 4, both 5 and 4 set a staggered screen on the weak side for 2.*

3. *2 has the ball at the top of the key, 5 clears out, 4 posts low on the ball side, 3 comes high and 1 slides to the corner on the weak side in case the offense decides to reverse the ball to try and post 5 low or run an inside screen away.*

4. *2 now has various options with the ball, including a pinch post or two-man game with 4 or 5.*

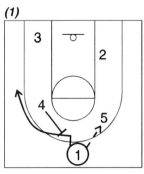

(1)

(2)

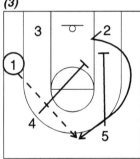

(3)

(4)

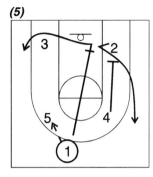

(5)

(6)

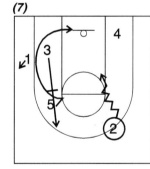

(7)

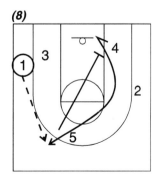

(8)

High post entry and double vertical screen down

5. *Normally, we want 1 to pass and screen and then the post man screens. This staggers the screen. 1 can cut inside or outside of 4 to set the first screen for 2. 1 then clears away in either direction to give 5 another passing option if he is unable to pass to 2. 1 may clear to the corner next to 2 if the defense doesn't permit him to cut opposite the ball.*

6. *5 can pass to 2 and receive a back-screen from 3 for the lob pass which gives 2 the opportunity to pass inside to 4, penetrate or reverse the ball to 3 who has stepped out. (See Diagram No. 7.)*

7. *If 5 passes to 1 with 3 posting, he would then screen diagonally down and away for 4, then pivot and post inside.*

8. *1 may pass to 3 inside on the block or to 4. 4 then looks inside to 5 and shoots, penetrates or passes to 2 on the weak side or to 3 who has interchanged with 1.*

** *It's important to remember that with the ball on the wing, in the post or on the perimeter, we always look for weak-side cuts.*

Selected Plays for the Box Offense
1-2-2 Offensive Alignment

1. Double screen away after a wing entry to either side by the point man. Wings may begin on elbows and then pop to the wings or they can begin on the wings. 1 enters to 2 and then cuts down the middle and uses a big-man screen to cut to the ballside corner. If he cuts away from the ball, 2 dribbles a-cross the court and the double screen is set on that side of the court for 1 by 3 and 5. 2 passes to 2 who has replaced 3 and he sets a double screen with 4 for 1.

2. After the pass to 1, 3 and 4 screen across the lane for 5 who waits until they screen his man before he cuts. 2 may penetrate or shoot instead of passing to 1 if he is open or he can play the two-man game or pinch post with 5.

3A. 1 cuts away and 4 comes up to set a two-man game scr-een for 3 on the wing.

3B. A screen up from the baseline provides a very good angle that is difficult to defend in this area of the court and provides good angles for the pen-etrate-and-pitch op-tions.

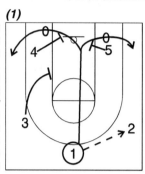
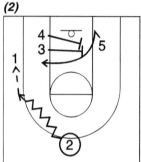
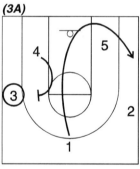

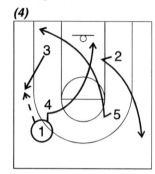

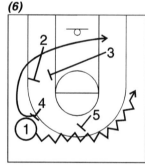

4. UCLA lob option for 1 after the weak-side lob clearout by 5. The Chicago Bulls use this with Michael Jordan or Scottie Pippen mak-ing the initial entry pass in the triple post offense and then looking for a lob pass or postup op-tion.

5. 3 has the ball as 2 clears out to the weakside wing area. 2 can also break quickly to the top of the key to look for a 3-point shot oppor-tunity. 1 must wait for 5 to clear out before running his man off of 4 to set up the lob pass. If the pass is not there, we pass to 2 and set up a triangle screening option by having 1 screen across on the low post for 5.

6. Misdirection for the high post scr-eener on the double high-staggered pick entry off the dribble. This second option is a difficult-to-de-fend, 5-to-2 diago-nal screen away.

7. If unable to pass to 4 on the misdirec-tion, we reverse the ball to the top for a shot or penetration for 2. We also have the option to reverse the ball to 5 posting up inside.

Selected Plays for the Box Offense
High post entry where the big men set up diagonally opposite high and low

1. Entry pass from 1 to 3 sets up a one-on-one chance for 3 as 1 cuts outside of 4 after the pass and 5 makes a quick diagonal cut clearing out away from the basket. 2 steps out to the weakside wing area and if 3 can't penetrate, 4 uses a backpick from 5 to dive to the strongside low post looking for a pass from 3.

2. 1 and 4 set baseline screens for 2 coming to the ball side. If 2 isn't open, he sets up other options by his movement. 3 passes to 5 and follows the ball for a handoff from 5 to penetrate or he reverses as 5 sets up the two-man game and 3 dribbles to get the ball to 2 in the corner once 3 dribbles back toward 2, 1 comes up and sets a backpick for 5 on the weak side for the lob in our misdirection action. (See Diagram No. 4)

3. Handoff for a screen-and-roll or a pass back to 5 stepping out.

4. A possible pass from 3 to 5 and then 2 uses a down-screen from 3, baseline screens by 4 and 1 or a post-up option for 4 stepping in before or after he screens.

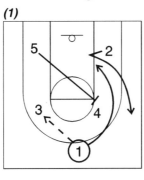
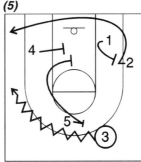

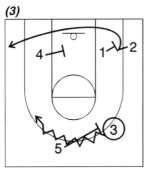

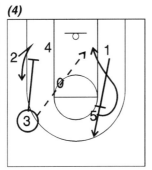

5. After the 3-5 two-man game, 5 and 4 can set a baseline double screen for 2 after a single baseline screen has been set for 2 by 1. 2 has the option to move from corner to corner depending on how the defense plays him. (See Diagram No. 3)

6. Here we have a zipper option not normally seen, but difficult to defend. On dribble penetration to the wing by 1, 4 and 5 vertically screen down and 3 comes up on a zipper move as 2 clears to the ball side and 1 passes to 2 in the corner or to 4 posting. If 4 is not open, 1 passes to 3 at the top of the key. 3 can penetrate, shoot or pass to 2. (See Diagram No. 7)

8. 3 passes to 2 and now 2 can penetrate or shoot from the wing. If he isn't open, 2 can pass inside to 5 or hit 4 flashing into the paint. 3 always has the option to look to reverse the ball to 1. 2 has the ball and we can see the passing angles and options he can use.

Selected Plays for the Box Offense
Double stack option off a dribble entry

1. 1 dribbles and enters the wing area as 5 and 3 screen in the lane for 2. Following his screen, 3 cuts diagonally up and across the lane as 4 makes a vertical cut to the weakside low block. 5 posts on the strongside block.

(1)
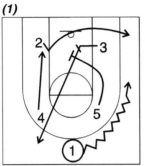

(4)
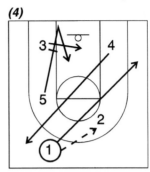

2. 1 has the ball on the wing and the players are in their positions after they have screened and cut, with 5 posting and 2 in the corner. If 4 breaks to the ball we can run a backdoor for 3. If 1 makes a direct pass to 3, 3 and 4 can run a two-man game or pinch post option.

3. If 1 elects to pass to 2 in the corner, he screens away and interchanges with 3. We also have 4 and 5 posting. 5 can also set a two-man game screen from the corner if 5 steps out to screen.

(2)

(5)

(3)

(6)
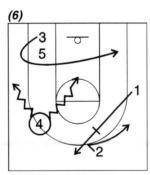

4. We have a 1 and 4 diagonal interchange without a screen. This creates better spacing for an entry pass to 2 playing the high post and then stepping out. As 4 reaches his spot above the elbow, 5 begins to walk his man down to screen for 3 on the low block. 2 may pass to 1, 4 or even 3 faking up and coming across the lane to the ball. In this case, 5 will reverse pivot and post up.

5. 2 makes his pass to 4 and 5 pins down on the man screening 3 as 3 fakes into the lane. 4 should be one step outside the elbow and above the circle, if possible, and 1 should be at the foul line extended for spacing and to set up a backdoor option if overplayed and 2 dribbles to 1's defender. Proper spacing is very important.

6. 4 receives from 2 and can penetrate or wait for 3 to circle 5 so 4 can dribble to the wing to look inside and post 5. 1 and 2 pick away or backpick on an interchange on the weak side. On timed reversal of the ball from 4-to-1-to-2 we have created another curl option for 3.

Selected Plays for the Box Offense
Final option in curl play from previous page

(7)

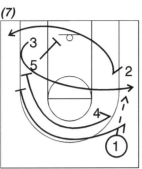

7. This diagram shows the cut in Diagram No. 6. We have 3 curling over 5 to the strongside wing and 2 crossing by cutting under 5 at the same time. This eliminates 2 and 3 switching equals on the cross. 1 passes to 3, then cuts away on the tail of 4 to set a triple staggered screen with 5 and 4 for 2.

(8)

8. 2 takes his man into the lane, then comes to the top of the key to receive the ball from 3. 4 continues to the block to post up after the screen has been used, thus giving another option to 3 who is also in position to penetrate.

(9)

9. 2 has the ball and can penetrate or shoot from the top of the key, or pass and cut to get us into our motion game. We now demonstrate over-and-under crossing action by the wings and penetration by 2.

(10)

(11)

(12)

(13)

10. The alignment in Diagram 11 shows that we can run any of the fundamental basketball options that we use in practice every day as well as our motion or free-lance game.

11. On the penetrating dribble by our point guard in our double stack offense, we run our zipper option. By starting out low, we give our wings more latitude in breaking to get free and also create great inside passing options when the defenders chase the wings.

12. The alignment with the wings wide and in the corners on the baseline, and the post men high, on or above the elbows, provides excellent pentrating angles for the point guard as well as optimum angles for backpicks, downscreens and lob plays. We can also post mismatches inside as we take away the help. Our 2-3 turnout action is also effective in this situation.

13. The 1-4 high set takes away pressure and gives us an opportunity to take advantage of the defense when we have a tall point man with good low post scoring ability.

135

Selected Plays for the Box Offense
Double Stack Options

Inverting the 2 and 3 and giving zipper action to the double stack

1. Diagonal screening action, which begins after sideline dribble penetration by 1 after 4 diagonally backscreens 2. 2 goes to the low block and waits for 4 to set a two-man game screen at the wing for 1. 1 changes direction or crosses over with his dribble and uses the screen to penetrate to the middle of the court.

2. When 1 passes 4, 5 goes down to screen 3 on the low block. 3 must bring his man into the lane and stop in order to provide 5 with an angle to screen 3's defender and then 3 moves to the wing area for a pass from 1 as 5 pivots and posts.

3. 3 has the ball and 2 can now cut baseline to the nearside corner for a pass from 3 which sets up a scissor option with 5 and 3.

4. 2 may elect to wait until 3 receives and then, on a double staggered screen set by 1 and 4, he can come back to the weakside looking for a spot-up pass from 3 as 3 penetrates.

** We can enter this play by crossing 3 and 4 on the transition from the wings.

(1)
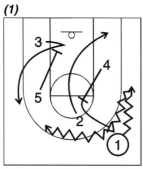

(2)

(3)
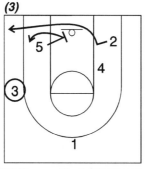

(4)

(5)
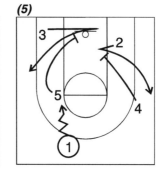

(6)

(7)
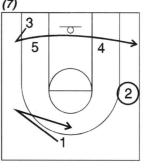

(8)
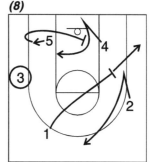

Double stack option after 2 and 3 cross on the baseline or simply fan to the corners on the transition.

5. 2 and 3 settle in the baseline area outside the free-throw lane in unbalanced positions to break out to receive the ball from 1, who is in the middle of the court after 4 and 5 go down and screen vertically.

6. On the entry pass to 2, 1 sets a screen away for 3 in a staggered stack alignment with 5. We again want 3 to take his man into the paint to allow 5 to headhunt the defender.

7. 3 may fake high and cut baseline to the ball side as 2 did in the previous play when the defense shaded him to the outside.

8. When 3 receives on the wing, 5 can post low and 1 and 2 interchange off the ball by screening for one another. If 5 can't post his man, he reverse pivots and screens across for 4.

Selected Plays for the Box Offense

Plays expressly designed to take advantage of a decided point guard height advantage or a point man's ability to post his defender. Of course, we also need a capable high post passer such as San Antonio's David Robinson.

1. *Our point passes to the high post and cuts around or in front of the other high post player to post in the lane. He may or may not rub his man off of a screen. 2 clears across on the entry pass to open the low post area.*

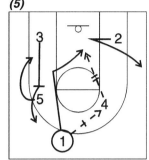

5. Another big guard posting entry: *High post entry pass to 4 stepping out. 2 clearing out to the wing and 3 waiting until 1 fakes the screen on 5 and posts in the middle before coming up to backpick 5's defender.*

2. *5 has the ball and 1 is posted inside with the shooter, 2, spotting up. We also show 1 with the option to come back up to backpick 4's defender. (See Diagram No. 3)*

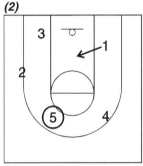

6. *4 with the ball and his options. He can post 1, pass to 2 and have 1 screen 5, pass to 3 and screen away with 2 for 1 coming out, pass to 5 stepping up, or penetrate and shoot.*

3 *We show 1 backpicking 4 and following the pass to 5 with 1 stepping out and 5 screening for 2 and then 3. Should 5 pass to 1 because 4 is covered inside, we have created a scoring chance for 2 or 3. If we reverse the ball, we can post 5 inside.*

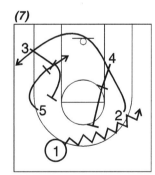

7. *Similar action for 1 with 2 and 3, and 4 and 5 in opposite high-low positions. 1 has the ball on the point and 2 immediately clears diagonally across the court off of 3's screen. After 2 cuts, 4 headhunts 1's defender in a two-man game play option. 1 can drive to the goal, 3 can set a screen for 2, then a backscreen for 5. 3 then steps out to the ball side as 4 screens him and then 2.*

4. *Final continuity with 5 and 4 posted low and penetrate-and/or-pitch opportunities for 1.*

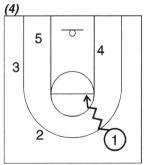

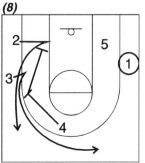

8. *Floor balance after all screens have been set.*

Selected Plays for the Box Offense

High post guard-around entry

Low double stack set

1. Point man passes to the high post and follows the ball to the wing area as the low post man on that side (2) clears across the lane and curls off of 3. On a switch, 3 can step in for the ball and an easy scoring opportunity if the switch is not perfectly executed. 1 has the option of making his cut under the post man if the defense tries to force him away.

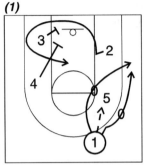

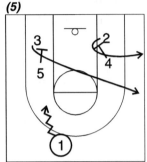

5. 4 screens down on 2 who circles over him to the corner. At the same time, 5 picks down on 3, enabling 3 to make a diagonal cut to the strongside high wing area. 1 can penetrate, work inside with 5 or pass to 3.

2. 2 has circled back to the strongside low post and 4 and 3 have interchanged on the weak side by either a pindown or backpick. 5 can pass to 3 or 4 if open, penetrate, shoot or look to the strongside screening action between 1 and 2.

6. 1 Has passed to 3 and cut away from the ball as 5 flashes to the high post area. This takes away the inside help on 4 and gives 3 a high-low option as well. 3 may also set up scissoring action with 2 and 4, or he can simply pass to 2, then cut to the basket.

3. 5 passes to 1 and then waits for 4 to set a diagonal backscreen on 5's defender. 1 can pass to either of the big men if open or to 2 on the low post. He also has the option of beckoning to 4 to set a screen.

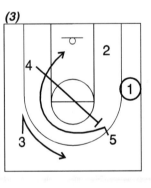

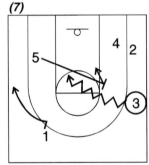

7. Another option is 5 continuing to set a two-man game screen-and-roll opportunity for 3. If 3 penetrates, he has 1 spotting up or in a position to cut backdoor.

4. 1 makes his entry pass to 4 on the high post, then flares off a backscreen set by 5 from the low post once 2 has been permitted to move and cut off of 3. 3 may step in on the switch as he screens. 4 has the option to pass to any of his teammates if they are free.

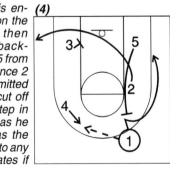

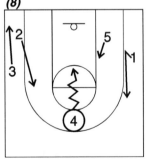

8. This diagram follows Diagram No. 4. Our 4 man has the ball at the top of the key. 5 has opted to remain on the low post instead of screening for 1, and 4 is isolated on the top. We can cross, flash for a backdoor or go into motion.

Selected Plays for the Box Offense
Curl and turnout option from the double stack set

1. *1 dribble penetrates to the wing as 2 curls inside and over 3 on the low block. 2 has options to cut under the double stack of 4 and 5 on the weak side or he may cut up and out to the weakside wing area. 4 reads 2 and moves in the opposite direction to get free.*

2. *On the curl by 2, we have 3 step in for the ball looking for a pass from 1.*

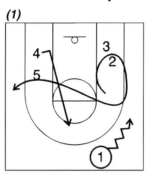

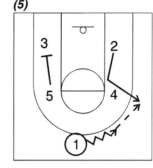

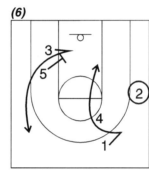

3. *3 can step to the corner to open up the court or go one-on-one when he receives the ball.*

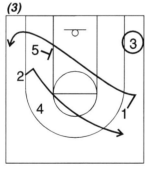

4. *If 3 has no one-on-one opportunity, he can pass to 5 flashing across the lane to the low post or pass to 2 who can reverse the ball. 3 can also set up our splitting-the-post option.*

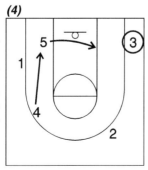

5. *UCLA entry option to the wing setting up an opportunity to make a lob pass to the cutting point guard or to post a point guard who has a height advantage or exceptional posting ability when the entry pass is made, 3 and 5 begin to come together on the weak side.*

6. *3 and 5 coming together take away the weakside help on 1, and as 3 breaks out, he gives us a passing option should the defense trap down or double 1. He passes to 4 and 4 looks to 3 on the weak side.*

7. *If 2 can't post 1, 4 can dive on 5 and we have 5 curling to the ball. 3 breaks to center field as another outlet for 2, and 1 releases to the corner to open up the court.*

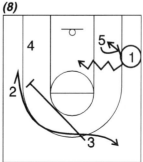

8. *2 has passed to 1 or 3 which gives us inside passing possibilities with 5, as well as a corner 5-1 two-man game. If the pass is to 3 and not 1, we can quickly reverse the ball or go into our pass-and-cut or motion options.*

Selected Plays for the Box Offense

(1)

1. The point passes to 5, then flares off of 4. At the same time, 2 clears low and across the lane off of 3 who steps in looking for the ball if the defense switches or if he feels he is open. Another strong option is a one-on-one chance for 5.

(5)

5. High double stack set for a delay game or crossing action to enter our 1-4 high set. 2 steps up inside 4 and reverse pivots to the basket for the lob as 3 steps to the wing to give us a UCLA entry if we don't have the lob pass to 4.

(2)
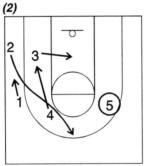

2. 5 has the one-on-one chance, 3 steps in and clears if he doesn't receive the ball, 4 dives low, and 1 and 2 can either interchange or screen on the weak side.

(6)
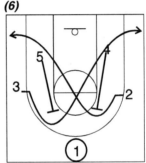

6. We break 4 and 5 to the high post areas as 2 and 3 cross and cut over the post men to the opposite corners giving us different entry options to begin the offensive play.

(3)

3. If 5 passes to 2, 3 is in position to set a backpick on 5's defender for the lob pass. 2 also is in position to penetrate, shoot, pass inside to 4, or pitch to 1 or 3.

*****Remember: We can place any of our better one-on-one players in any of the five positions to take advantage of the one-on-one scoring option.*

4. On the pass to 1,
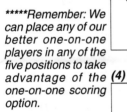
4 is posted low with 2 and 3 screening and interchanging off the ball on the weak side. The movement of 2 and 3 occupies the help defense and provides floor balance.

(4)
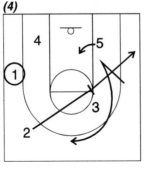

(7)
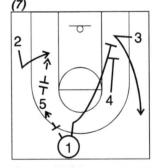

7. Alignment after the crossing action in the previous diagram. This creates another situation the defense must contend with. 1 passes to 5 and sets a vertical double staggered downscreen for 3 with 4. At the same time, 2 fakes up to the wing and, if overplayed, cuts backdoor to the goal looking for a pass from 5.

(8)
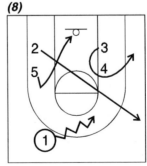

8. Quick-hitting double stack backdoor lob entry for the 5 man after 2 vacates the low post area to isolate 5. Defense must follow 2 because he is a shooting guard and a scoring threat.

Selected Plays for the Box Offense
UCLA Set

(1)
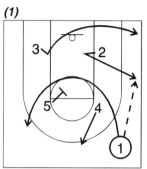

1. On entry pass to 2 breaking high to the wing area, 3 clears baseline to the strongside corner. 1 first cuts off a screen by 4, then another by 5 and continues to the weakside wing area at approximately the elbow extended.

(2)

2. With the ball in his hands, 2 passes to 4 stepping out after his screen of 1, and 4 reverses the ball to 1 on the wing. 5 fights for low post position for a pass from 1 and 2 cuts to the block or picks away and interchanges with 3. 4 dives low or cuts after his pass.

(3)

3. On a pass to the corner by 2, he executes a give-and-go and if 3 has no one on one opportunity, 4 goes and sets a screen in the corner for 3 in a pick-and-roll option. 1 fills above the top of the key for defensive balance.

(4)

4. On the penetration by 3, 4 rolls or steps back and our other players spot up to establish passing lanes, prepare for three-point shot opportunities and to be in position to rotate the ball against trapping defenses.

(5)
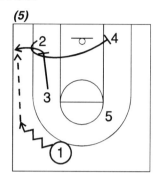

5. On 1's dribble entry to the wing in our unbalanced box, 3 screens down for 2 on the ball or strong side, and 2 curls over 3 and across the lane to screen for 4 as 3 steps to the corner. If 2 is open, he'll receive a pass from 1, but this passing angle is difficult because the cutter is moving away from the ball. 3 also has a one-on-one play from the corner.

(6)
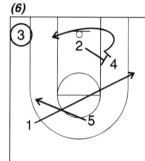

6. 3 has the ball and looks inside for 4 crossing the lane after his pick from 2 (small-on-big). 1 cuts away and interchanges with 5. 4 may continue to the corner to screen for 3 with the ball.

(7)
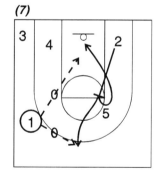

7. If 1 doesn't cut and either can't pass in the corner to 3, or if he receives a return pass from 3, he looks for 2 to set a backpick on 5's defender. This sets up a lob pass to 5 or a pass to 2 stepping out following his screen.

(8)
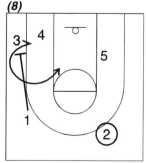

8. If the pass is made to 2, 1 sets a screen away for 3 who can curl or step out. 2 may also penetrate or play pinch post with 5.

Selected Plays for the Box Offense

Zipper set with the post men diagonally opposite one another. We can put 3 and 5 in a low stack on the weak side and still be in the box offense.

1. 1 dribbles to side-line and that's the signal for 4 to diagonally pick up on 2 who waits until the screen is set before cutting. 4 steps out after the screen and when 4 receives the ball ...

2. 5 pins down on 3 and 4 passes to 3 coming up. We don't want 5 to screen until 4 has received the pass from 1. In Diagram No. 1 our first option is 2 cutting or posting up. Once 4 passes to 3 or to 5 posting inside, he goes down and sets a screen for 2 on the baseline. 2 reads the screen. If overplayed he can cut to the strongside corner off 5 posting up.

3. Our next option is 2 cutting across before interchanging with 4. 3 passes back to 4 if 3 has no shot. Then 3 and 5 set a staggered baseline double screen for 2. To run a particular option, we can read the defense or use a predetermined signal or key. In our continuity in Diagram No. 3, 4 passes to 1 then screens down for 3 in a triangle move. By screening for 3, we take away a 2-3 switch.

4. After screening for 3, 4 dives to the ballside low post. Either he or 3 can receive a pass from 1, or 1 can penetrate to the goal.

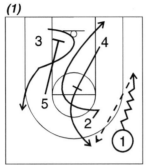

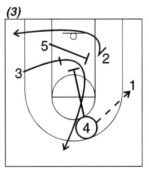

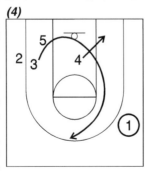

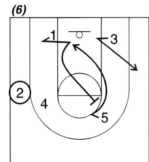

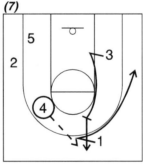

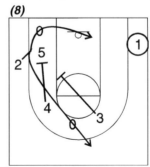

5. This play incorporates the UCLA set and what NBA personnel refer to as Atlanta, Utah, and now Houston, diagonal screening and cutting. We show the UCLA standard wing entry and guard cut off of the high post. The side of 4 the guard cuts on is determined by whether his defender goes over or under the screen.

6. We now look for misdirection action to post 5. If 1 decides the pindown or backscreen with 2 is not there after 2 sees 1 is not free on the initial cut and passes to 4 stepping out, 1 sets a diagonal small-to-big backpick for 5.

7. If 4 is unable to pass inside to 5, he fakes a pass and waits until 3 has an angle to backpick 1 on the weak side. 1 or 4 can also drive and shoot or, if they aren't free, pass back to 2 or 3 stepping out.

8. If 4 passes 1 or 3 on the weakside wing, he screens away for 2 and with 1 or 3 and 2 can come high off the double or fake high and cut baseline off of 5. If 2 cuts high, 4 or 5 have the option of cutting to the ballside low post. Whoever gets there first controls the low post position.

Selected Plays for the Box Offense
Zipper options

1. *Quick-hitting play inverting the 3 and 4 positions. 1 dribble penetrates to sideline on entry; 4 posts low as first option. 3 steps out from high post, receives pass from 1 and, as 3 catches ball, 5 screens down on 2, popping out in almost a brush block maneuver enabling 2 to catch ball and quickly penetrate to goal as other players spot up.*

The next 3 diagrams illustrate one of the most common box plays.

2. *Two differences: 3 and 5 are inverted and we take away defensive help or switching from weak side by sending 3 to strongside corner to free 2 or 3. This is a misdirection backpick by 5 for 2, and then 3 and 4 set a double screen for 2 breaking high.*

3. *Ball is in point's hands on wing. We have strongside triangle set and opportunity for 4 to backpick 2, screen for 1 or set up various flash backdoor or pinch post options.*

4. *If 1 passes to 2 for shot at top of key he can cut to opposite side of court or screen away for 3. If he passes to 3 he can cut or screen away for 2. 3 can pass inside, shoot, reverse ball or run a pick-and-roll from corner with 5. Other option is 4 flashing high if 5 is fronted from baseline side where we run high-low option.*

5. *Special option to set up misdirection screen for 3. 1 dribble penetrates to the side, with or without screen from 5. 1 may also run same action using guard-around entry with 5. After seeing 1 dribble by 5, 2 clears across baseline and gets screen from 3. 4 and 5 then go to baseline area to set double screen on 3's defender. This also takes care of any 2-3 switching that might have been called by the defense.*

6. *We now show 3 receiving ball in the corner. In this set, after 3 has screened and goes to the corner, 4 may curl back to low post off 5, an unexpected move difficult to defend.*

7. *3 has ball in corner; as he dribbles away from basket or penetrates, 4 screens away for 2 who is coming counterclockwise back across lane. 5 goes diagonally away to set backpick on 1's defender which sets up a lob or skip pass option to the weak side without defensive help. 2 is also free for field-goal attempt in corner as 4 posts low.*

8. *If 3 keeps his dribble alive we have a pick-and-roll option with 5 or even a handback option, if necessary. On penetration, our other players are spotted up. Defense is spread making trapping more difficult.*

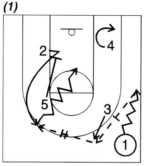

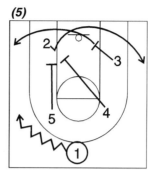

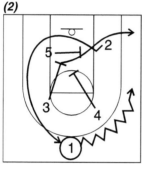

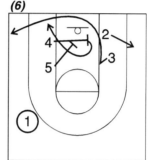

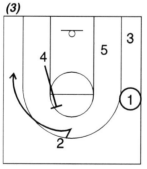

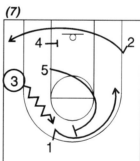

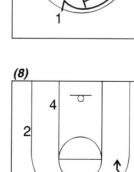

Selected Plays for the Box Offense
Pick-the-picker

Zipper entries

1. *5 screens 1 on high post pick-and-roll entry to relieve defensive pressure on 1. 3 then comes up lane to screen 5's defender giving 1 an "iso" play, then a lob to 5 cutting or a low post option with 5 as 3 steps out to open up the court and provide an outlet pass option.*

2. *3 receives ball at the high post, and in the triple threat position he can drive to the goal, shoot or wait for the screen by 4 on 2, and either pass to 2 popping out or 4 on low post after he has screened 2's defender and then his own defensive man. He also has option to pass back to 1 or 5 who can come up to meet the ball.*

3. *If 3 passes to 2 he can cut or receive backpick from 1 on weak side. 2 is in triple threat position and can dribble to corner to establish best passing angle to post 4 on block. He can also look for 3 after backpick or 1 who steps out after screening.*

4. *2 reverses ball to 1 and 1 passes to 3 where we have a number of options available if we cannot post 5, including the high-low with 4.*

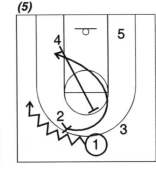
(1)

(2)

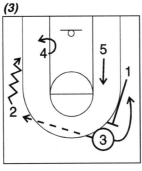
(3)

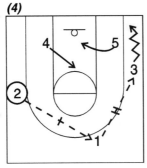
(4)

(5)

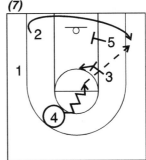
(6)

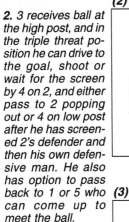
(7)

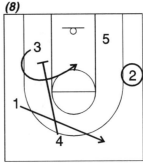
(8)

Zipper option

5. *Incorporates a good play to deter a team switching the 2 and 3 in a double stack. The key is putting 3 on top instead of below 5 in the baseline stack. 2 sets high screen for 1 to enter the wing and then, as in the previous play, the low post player comes up and back-picks the picker.*

6. *1 has option to pass to 2 on the block (2 may also fan out to the corner which enables 1 to cross over, drive and penetrate) or to pass to 4 stepping out. If 5 thinks his defender is cheating to help on the low post, he can flash post into the lane to the ball.*

7. *On the pass to 4 on the high post, 3 and 5 set a double pick on the baseline for 2 who reverses and comes back to the ball; 4 penetrates or brings ball to right side of court. If 3's defender tries to switch out into the passing lane over 3, 3 steps into the lane looking for a pass. This option usually catches the defense napping.*

8. *If 4 passes to 2, we have 5 posted as 3 clears across the lane and 4 dives to the boards to rebound. 3 can curl and come back into the lane for ball. 1 covers back to give defensive balance.*

Selected Plays for the Box Offense
Zipper pick-the-picker options with varied screening

1. *2 backscreens 1 at the high post and then 4 comes up to backpick 2 who this time goes directly to the corner (the key for 3) instead of posting on the block. Now 3 backpicks 5, setting up the lob from 1 on the weak side of the court. 1 has the option to make the lob pass to 5, penetrate, pass to 3 stepping out or pass to 2 in the corner.*

2. *The ball is in the corner on the pass to 2, 1 may stay or interchange with 4; 2 looks inside to 5, drives or shoots. If these options are not available, reverse ball around perimeter and look for 2 making a flex cut off 5 screening on the low post.*

3. Option for Diagram No. 1: *We have 2 faking the screen, stepping up and cutting to the corner after 1 penetrates to the wing. 2 may cut low off 4's pick or directly bury in the corner. 3 breaks to the high post on the ball side and 5 goes backdoor. On a pass to 3, we can go high-low with 4.*

4. Option after 3 and 5 interchange: *5 can come right back to the ball and we can go high-low to 4 as 3 fans out to the weakside wing.*

(1)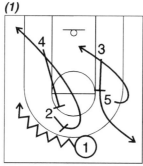

(2)

(3)

(4)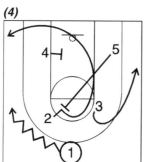

(5)

(6)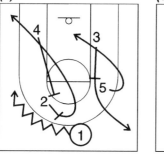

(7)

(8)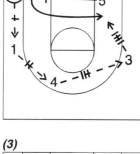

5. Normal Zipper with options: *1 dribble penetrates to wing and 4 screens down to the block as 2 waits for screen to be set before he moves to top of court to center field. 4 moves to low post as 2 or 3 steps outside the free-throw lane. 5 screens down on 3 who also waits for the screen and 5 immediately steps in and posts to the ball and a pass from 2.*

6. Option: *If 3 is overplayed and unable to cut high when 2 has the ball, 5, 4 and 1 set a triple staggered screen for 3 on baseline as 2 dribbles ball to right side of court to get 3 the ball.*

7. *On pass to 3, 2 moves away; 4 and 1 screen 5 on left side of the paint. 5 cuts baseline back to ball and 1 screens 4's defender, allowing 4 to curl toward the middle and come back to ball providing another option for 3 and the high-low possibility. 1 continues to corner and can interchange with 2.*

8. *If 3 is not free or if the defense forces him back to his left, he can pass to 1 stepping to the corner after screening 4 and we can post 4 inside as 2 and 3 interchange.*

****We must emphasize that screeners must take a step or two out after they screen to open the floor for proper spacing. **These players must see the ball and create passing lanes.***

Selected Plays for the Box Offense

Triple staggered screens for shooters with entry on either side of the court

1. 1 uses a dribble entry to the wing area off a high post screen set by 5. At the same time, 2 vacates the strong-side low post area and uses a triple staggered screen set consecutively by 3, 4 and then 5 as he comes to center field to receive a pass from 1 if 1 has not penetrated to the basket. After screening, 3 can post low or continue to the strongside corner. 4 and 5 move to positions once 3 makes his decision.

2. Same movement as in Diagram No. 1 but without the high post screen- and-roll entry.

3. 1 has the option to pass to 3 in the low post or back to the top to 2. 1 may also look for 4 flashing into the paint to take away the weakside help when 3 posts.

4. On the pass to 2, 1 screens for 3, 4 continues to the low post and 1 uses screens on the baseline from 4 and 5 to move to the other side of the court. We are now in a 1-2-2 set and 2 has any number of options in his arsenal.

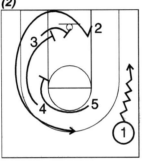

(1)

(2)

(3)

(4)

(5)

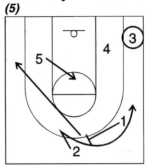

(6)

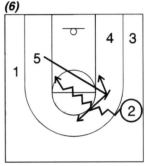

(7)

(8)

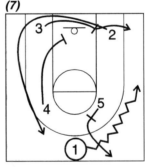

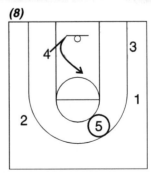

5. If 2 passes to 3 and 3 takes ball to corner, he can pass to 4 in low post and/ or have 4 pivot to screen away for 5. He can also penetrate or have 4 or 5 screen for him in corner for a two-man game. As this occurs, 1 screens away for 2 or 2 backpicks 1 to create the interchange off of the ball.

6. 3 passes ball back to 2, 5 breaks across court to set a two-man game screen for 2 on the wing. He (5) can also break high to set up pinch post option for 2. If 5 receives pass from 2 he can look in for the high-low option with 4 or he can look for 3 making flex cut on baseline using a screen set by 4. 3 reads and cuts over or under, according to how the defense plays his cut.

7. Option: 1 dribbles off screen by 5 and 5 steps back instead of going to screen for 3. 1 passes back to 5 and they look for a give-and-go or backdoor play, or 5 looks for 2 coming off stag-gered double screen set by 3 and 4.

8. 3 continues to corner. If 2 is covered, 5 can pass inside to 4 posting to meet the pass or have 2 screen 3 across the lane or 2 screen his own defender to free himself and his teammate.

Selected Plays for the Box Offense

Staggered set with both big men on the same side of the floor

1. Special play with options: 1 moves to the wing area with the dribble. He may or may not use the screen from 5. 4 posts low and asks for the ball on the entry and 3 comes diagonally across the lane from the low block to set a backpick on 5's defender to set up the lob pass option from 1. 2 fakes and fades to the weakside wing.

2. If the lob pass or low post opportunity is not there, 1 can pass to 3 and get a pass back and then 3 will move to the corner. The move by 3 can be a give-and-go cut down the lane and around 4 or he can execute a bury cut to the corner. As 3 cuts through, 1 uses his cut as a brush block and penetrates with the ball as 2 and 5 spot up to get free and to move the defense.

3. 1 passes to 3 in the corner instead of penetrating and he cuts to the other side of the court or sets a screen away for 2. 4 goes to the corner for a two-man game option with 3.

4. 3 penetrates, 4 rolls or steps back and the other players move to set passing lanes for the player with the ball.

(1)
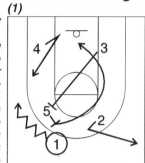

(2)
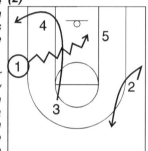

(3)
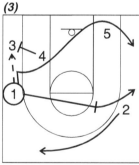

(4)
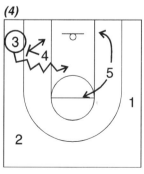

(5)

(6)
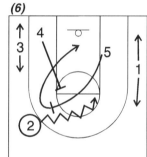

(7)
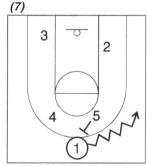

(8)

5. 3 passes to 2 on the interchange between 1 and 2 and 2 can penetrate or use 5 coming high for a pinch post or two-man game. If 4 is being fronted, he can seal his man for the high-low after a direct pass from 2 to 5 near the elbow area. On the reversal of the ball, 3 can run a flex cut off of 4 on the baseline.

6. Pick-and-roll penetration between 2 and 5 as the other players spot up. Some NBA teams use a backscreen by 4 on 5's defender to help 5 roll to the basket after 2 dribbles by the screen and begins to penetrate. Many teams use this as a last second need play.

7. Dribble penetration entry by 1 after a high screen by 5.

8. Pass back to the screener stepping out and then a back-pick by 3 for 1. 5 can lob to 1 or pass to 4 posting from the weak side.

Selected Plays for the Box Offense
Diagonal backscreen series

Box 1-4 high versus pressure

1. 1 receives a high pick-and-roll screen from 4 and dribbles to an area below the wing. 2 clears out the area on the dribble and circles diagonally up to set a backscreen on 5's defender. 5 cuts over or under the screen depending on how he is defended. 3 clears to the corner and 2 then backpicks 4 and steps out.

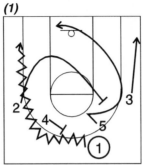
(1)

2. 1 looks for a pass to 5 coming to the strongside block or to 4 following 2's backpick. He can also pass to 2 or have 2 come to him to set a screen off of the dribble. 4 can also downscreen 2.

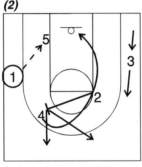
(2)

3. If 1 passes to 2 or 4, if the latter doesn't use 2's screen, 3 fakes up and cuts backdoor if he is being overplayed. 4 may also penetrate or pass the ball around the perimeter and then either cut or screen away.

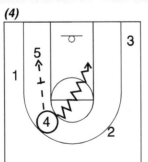
(3)

4. 4 can play high-low with 5 or penetrate to the goal and pitch if his drive to the basket is stopped.

(4)

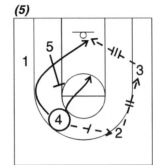
(5)

5. Continuity: If 4 elects to reverse the ball, 5 can come up to backpick 4's defender and 4 can cut behind or over the screen, depending upon how the defense plays him.

6. 1 uses a dribble entry to the wing. He can opt to use or not use the screen being set by 5. 2 is on the weakside block and can elect to clear baseline to the strong side or fake and step out to the weak side. 3 sets a diagonal backscreen for 4 and steps out as 5 did after 1 passed him on the dribble. 1 looks for the lob to 4 or 4 on the low post.

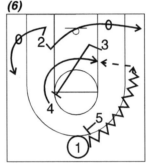
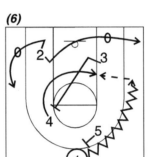
(6)

7. 3 continues and backpicks for 5 and 2 spots up. 1 passes to 4 and interchanges with 3. If 4 is trapped, he swings the ball to 2 who has established a passing lane for him and we look to move the defense by reversing the ball.

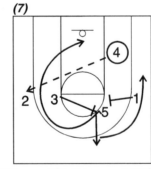
(7)

8. When we reverse the ball, we look for our post men screening for each other on the low post. After the screen is set, we have the screener turn opposite the cutter and back to the ball.

Selected Plays for the Box Offense
End-of-game or special need situation plays: Misdirection action

1. *1 passes to 4 on the weakside high post and at the same time 3 cuts diagonally to the weakside corner. 1 follows the ball and looks for the handback from 4. He can also cut under 4 to the wing area if he is denied over-the-top access.*

2. *On the handoff or pass from 4 to 1, 4 pivots and sets a two-man game pick for 1 which enables 1 to penetrate to the middle or drive back to the left wing area. 3 uses screens on the baseline by 2 and then 5, to run his man to the ball. This may force a big-to-small switch. 4 steps back or goes down to screen 2 on the weak side.*

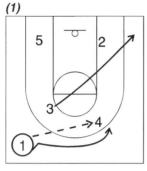

(1)

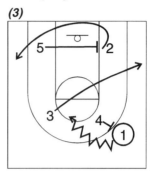

(3)

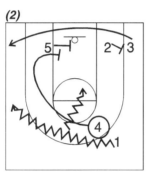

(2)

(4)

3. *On the screen-and-roll between 4 and 1, 3 moves directly across to corner opposite point guard's entry. 1 can penetrate the middle, pass to 4 stepping back or rolling to goal, or look for 2, who waits until 5 crosses lane to set baseline screen for him as he comes to ball. We have created a possible defensive switch of unequal-sized players.*

4. *Same as No. 3, but 3 circles 5 and sets first staggered screen for 2 and then 5 screens 2's defender whether it's the defensive 2 or 3 man. If forced sideline, 1 can penetrate. 1-to-4 pick-and-roll option is now wide open.*

Special plays

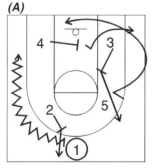

(A)

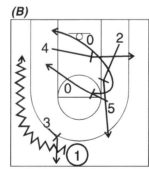

(B)

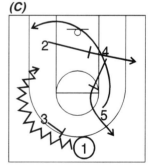

(C)

A. 2 and 3 lined up diagonally opposite. The defense must decide which of the two screens it should switch or if it should body check and stay. 2 screens for 1 who tries to bring the ball down to the corner for 5 who has used two backpicks, first from 3 and then from 4 across the lane, to get to the ballside block. 5 can make his cut over or under to establish position by reading the defense.

B. We have switched 3 and 2 and 1 again enters to the wing and corner. We must remember that 3 may or may not screen 1's defender and then step out. 2 Then backpicks 5, then 4 does the same. By crossing the lane, 2 continues and screens 3 off of the ball.

C. 2 and 3 are now on the same side, forcing a switching team into the small-big switch. If 5 goes to the corner instead of posting up, he gives 1 a great opportunity to penetrate to the goal as 2 clears to what is now the weakside corner.

Selected Plays for the Box Offense

Double screen options with continuity

Double backscreen for the big man with pick-the-picker misdirection

1. *1 enters on a sideline dribble as 3 screens across the lane and 5 picks diagonally across to the baseline setting a double screen for 2 breaking to the ballside corner. 4 begins to screen down on the side of the lane in pick-the-picker action for 3 continuing out.*

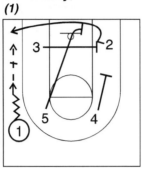

2. *1 passes to 2 in the corner, but he also has the option to drive to the goal or to hesitate and look inside for a big man or to the weak side for 3 circling.*

3. *2 has the ball to shoot or penetrate or to look for 4 coming to the ball in the low post after using a screen set by 5. 1 screens 3 to interchange and create outlets should the ball be reversed to the other side of the court. We also have provided very good penetrating options from all areas of the court.*

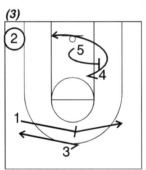

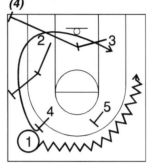

4. *Two consecutive high pick-and-roll screens for the point man who has the option of crossing over and penetrating at any time once the dribbler passes 4, 2 comes up to set a vertical back screen on 4's defender and 3 starts across the lane to set a second backpick for 4.*

5. *After 1 passes 5, 4 is one option for 1 on the low post and another option is 5 screening for 2 coming up as 3 continues to the corner as an outlet. 1 passes to 2 and 2 can, penetrate, shoot or, as he does here, pass to 3 in the corner. 5 can post low or continue across the lane to screen 4 coming back to the ball.*

6. *After passing to 3, 2 can cut to the basket (give-and-go) or screen away for 1. The give-and-go should be executed as a "V" or banana cut.*

Coach's Edge
Our screening action is designed to create mismatches if the defense switches to stop the effectiveness of the play or if we are playing a team that normally switches every time the opposition crosses.

Selected Plays for the Box Offense

Two options for the big-man slash

(1)

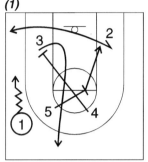

1. Point dribbles the ball to the wing and the 2 man cuts across the baseline using a screen from 3. Once 2 clears 3, 5 sets a diagonal screen away for 4 who cuts to the block to screen 3 coming up the lane. 1 Has the option to throw the lob pass to 5 who has split the defenders X4 and X5.

(2)

2. 3 cuts high to receive the pass from 1. The other options for 1 are 2 in the corner and 4 on the low post or as previously mentioned, the lob to 5. 3 receives the pass and he can penetrate to the goal. 2 may interchange with 1 or come back to the ball using baseline screens from 4 and 5. Both big men step to the ball after they pick.

(3)

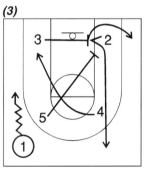

3. Slash action with the low post player clearing opposite the point's penetrating dribble entry. As 3 clears across the lane, 5 picks away for 4 and 4 dives to the ballside block. 5 picks across and 2 cuts high off 5's screen or to the corner and 3 goes to the other vacant area.

(4)

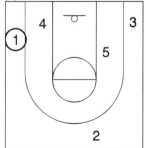

4. 4 should be free, but if he is not, 1 can drive, penetrate and pitch or pass back to the top to 2 or 5.

Buttonhook options for wing after dribble penetration or handback

(5)

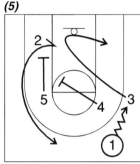

5. 1 penetrates the wing area and 3 clears diagonally across the lane and suddenly stops to freeze his defender. He then pivots back to the ball, sealing his defender behind him. 4 and 5 screen across the lane for 2.

(6)

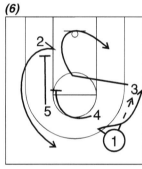

6. 1 passes to 3, fakes away and comes back for a handback. 3 gives the ball back to 1 and does the same thing as in diagram no. 5. 4 and 5 again set a double staggered screen away for 2 who comes to center field.

(7)

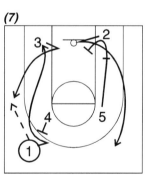

7. Flex continuity action: 1 passes to 3 on the wing and makes a UCLA vertical cut off of a screen by 4. When 4 receives a pass from 3, 5 pins down on 2 and then pivots and posts. 2 may also backpick 5 in the same process. 4 can pass to 5 posting or to 2 coming up on a zipper move.

(8)

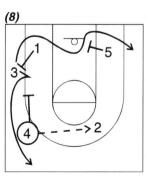

8. When 4 passes to 2, 1 backpicks 3 and 3 can use the screen by 1 and a screen by 5 to cut baseline to the opposite corner. If he uses the screen by 1 and cuts baseline, 1 and 4 screen vertically for each other, either up or down as in the normal flex offense.

Selected Plays for the Box Offense

1-4 High set with backdoor options vs. defensive pressure on the wings

Yugoslavian option for Tony Kukoc (High Post)

1. 1 dribbles toward 3, recognizes the overplay and drives ball at the leg of 3's defender as 3 fakes to the ball and reverses sharply to the goal to receive a bounce pass from 1. The dribble at the defender is important because it freezes the defender. If the backdoor is not there, 5 can step back or screen for 1.

2. 1 makes the entry pass to 4, the weakside high post man, and 2 fakes to the ball and cuts backdoor for a drop pass from 4. We would like the pass to be a bounce pass because it's easier for 2 to see and more difficult to defend. 1 follows his pass the same as he does in our pinch post series.

3. 5 and 3 pin down on the weak side for 2 if he has not received the backdoor pass. This provides 4 with an additional option. 4 can also take his defender one-on-one.

4. After 2 cuts to the wing, 3 can curl to the middle around 5, 4 can penetrate or pass to 2 or 1. If he passes to 1, he can go and screen away for 5 or cut to the basket.

(1)

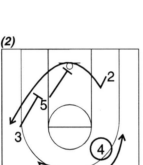
(2)

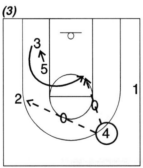
(3)

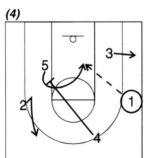
(4)

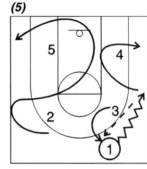
(5)

(6)

(7)

(8)

5. 1 dribbles to the wing area and the high post player on that side steps out to center field. We now can pass to 3 stepping out or we can look inside to our low post player. On a pass to the high post, 1 and the other wing (2) cross or curl off of the low post men. Our rule is that 2 follows the lead of the passer and makes the same cut that 1 does. In this manner the defense can't anticipate what we will do. The first option is for 3 to go one-on-one.

6. In this diagram, the guards cross after the entry pass. In Diagram No. 5 they come out the same side corner. In both cases, the low post men screen and post and on a drive by 3 they curl and establish outlet passing lanes for 3.

7. Dribble penetration by 3 with curls and spotting up to establish passing lanes.

8 Pindown-and-post or upblock-and-cut options which are determined by how the defense tries to play our offensive movement.

Selected Plays for the Box Offense

"High post" play (Continued)	High post pass entry and flare cut

(1)

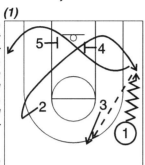

1. Dribble entry to wing with high post step out to center field for a pass. It's important that 3 steps out to the ball side to eliminate the crosscourt pass and set up the backdoor if he is pressured.

2. We are setting up a double screen option for 3 which occurs if we do not have the one-on-one option from the high post area. 3 dribbles to the other side of the court and passes to 1 who has crossed under 5 to this spot. 3 then screens down for 5 and goes away and gets a double screen on the other side of the lane from 4 and 2. 1 may pass to 5 or run a wing two man game with 5 to penetrate or bring the ball to 3. This also helps to keep the ball in our best distributors' hands.

3. 1 has passed to 3 and 4 comes back to the ball by curling around a screen in the lane by 2. 2 continues to the corner.

4. 3 has the option to penetrate, pass to 4 inside or pitch to 1 who has worked his way back to the top as 5 dives to rebound on the weak side.

(2)

(3)

(4)

(5)

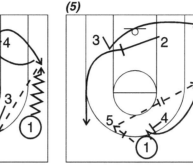

5. 1 passes to the high post and moves opposite off a backpick from the weakside high post. 5 can throw a skip pass back to 1 or he can pass to 4 stepping out who then can pass to 1. On the return pass to 1, 2 comes across the lane to screen for 3. If 3 does not receive a pass he continues to the corner.

(6)

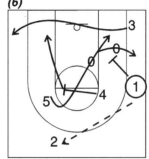

6. 1 waits for 4 to screen across for 5 and if 5 is not free, 1 passes back to 2 circling to the ball. On this pass, 1 screens down on 5 and 3 cuts back across the baseline.

7. 2 looks for penetration, a shot or a pass to 3. If those options aren't there, he waits for 5 to step out after the pick from 1. 1 continues through the lane and sets a small-on-big pick in the lane for 4 coming to the ball. 1 continues to the corner.

(7)

(8)

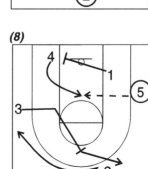

8. 5 looks inside for 4 as 2 and 3 interchange for defensive balance, for passing outlets and to take away defensive help.

***Note: We can place any players in any of the offensive positions to place additional pressure on the defense.

Selected Plays for the Box Offense

Diagonal downscreening action	Double vertical screens for baseline shooters

1. *1 penetrates to the wing with or without screen from 4. Once 1 passes 4 on dribble, 4 goes down and diagonally screens for 3 who comes to high post. If switch occurs, 4 should pivot to ball to post up in lane. 1 can also pass to 2 down on the block or in the corner or to 3.*

(1)

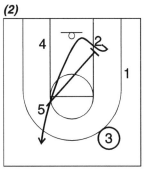

(5)

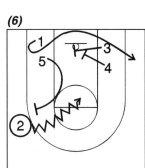

5. *1 passes to 4 on opposite high post and cuts outside or inside 5 to set vertical downscreen for 2. 5 waits for 1 to pass him and sets a second staggered vertical screen for 2. 3 posts low; 4 passes to 3 or 2.*

2. *3 receives ball near or above the 3-point line. When this pass is made, 5 diagonally downscreens for 2 coming to the 3-point area. 3 can pass to 2 for a scoring opportunity or pass back to 1 and 1 can pass inside to 5. If 2 dribbles to the wing, we post 4 or he screens for 5.*

(2)

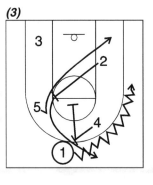

(6)

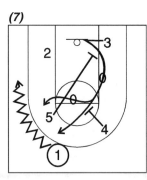

6. *4 passes to 2 who shoots, penetrates or waits for 5 to come up and set screen for our two-man game. 4 screens down with 3 on the weak side. 1 waits a count, then uses a 3-4 double screen on baseline as 2 dribbles across and 3 clears out.*

3. Diagonal backscreen: *1 dribbles to wing with or without a screen from 4. As he passes by 4, 2 screens diagonally up on 5 and 5 cuts to the ballside low post as 4 picks the picker (2) who steps out to the ball. 1 looks to 5 inside, 4 on a lob play or he passes to 2.*

(3)

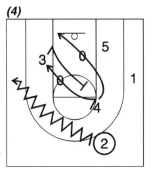

(7)

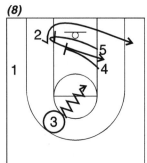

7. Diagonal downscreen option: *1 dribbles to wing with or without a high post screen. 5, the nearside post man, then diagonally screens down and away for 3 coming up to ball. 1 looks inside, drives or passes to 3 and, at the same time, 4 goes down to set double screen with 5.*

4. *2 has the ball and dribbles to wing as 3 sets diagonal upblock for 4 who dives to the post. 3 steps out as an additional outlet if 4 is not free. 4 can also screen across the lane for 5 in our continuity and inside out and in action.*

(4)

(8)

8. *3 receives pass from 1 and dribble penetrates as 2 clears across the lane using the 4-5 double screen. If free, 2 gets ball for shot in the corner and 4 continues to set another pick for 5 across the lane coming back to the ball. 3 moves away.*

Selected Plays for the Box Offense

Zipper options

1. 1 penetrates the wing and weakside postman goes down and diagonally picks for strongside low post player who fakes and comes up above three-point line to receive a pass from 1. 4 posts up inside after he screens.

2. 3 catches pass and looks for shot, an offensive move or he penetrates to wing area which is signal for 2 on low block to come up diagonally across lane to backpick 5's defender enabling him to dive for position on low post. 2 steps out after setting screen to provide another outlet for 3 if 5 isn't open.

3. Zipper option if 2 is denied high weakside cut. 4 screens down on 3 and 1 passes to 3 and cuts horizontally across to weak side of court. When 3 gets ball, 2 fakes up and uses second screen set by 4 to come baseline to the strong side. He is usually free for a shot from corner. If defense switches the screen, we can go inside to 4.

4. One-on-one option for 3 after pass from 5 or triple screen opportunity for 2. 2 uses staggered triple to free himself. When 2 gets ball, 1 cuts to either corner and big men screen across for each other inside.

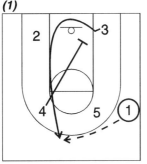

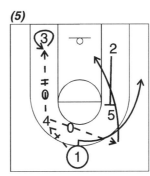

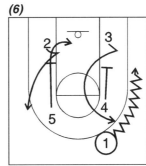

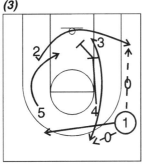

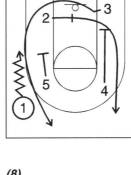

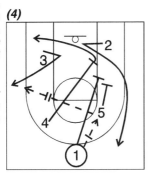

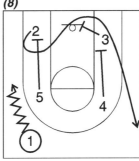

5. Special situation final play post-up option: 1 passes to high post and clears his man away opposite ball on a guard-around move over or under the other high post defender. 3 fakes to outside on low post and establishes low post position for pass from 4. 3 can reverse pivot for lob and 5 screens down on 2 for 3-point shot option. Best post player is down low on the left-hand block

6. Zipper option off dribble without screen: We only screen down two steps instead of going to the block to make low post players move defenders up lane from low post and give them an opportunity to go backdoor on an aggressive overplay.

7. Misdirection zipper options: 1 dribbles to wing; 4 and 5 partially pin down toward low posts. 2 either screens across lane for 3 or fakes the screen and goes to corner. 3 comes across the lane and zippers up off 5. 4 posts low or pins down on 2 should 2 cross the lane and zipper up for a pass from 3. Both 4 and 5 are inside threats!!!!

8. Double screen option off curl: 1 penetrates to wing; strongside post man screens down as in normal zipper. 2 waits for screen and curls around 5 to opposite low post off double screen set by 3 and then 4. 1 can pass to 5 after curl, penetrate and/ or bring the ball to 2.

Selected Plays for the Box Offense

Special zipper option

European handback option for the 1-4 high box offensive set

1. Pass and return pass between 1 and 2 after 2 receives wing entry pass. On first pass, both post players go to blocks on their respective sides of court, 5 establishes staggered double screen with 3 for 2, who after passing ball back to 1, cuts across court and under screen as 1 dribbles to penetrate or pass to 2 or 5.

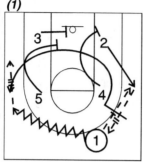

2. Variation of the UCLA from 1-4 High: First pass from 1 to 3 on wing and 1 cuts down off high post screen, hesitates, then curls back to top of key around downscreen by 5. 3 can drive to basket, run a two-man game with 5, pass to 4 posting after he screens down on 2 or pass back to 1.

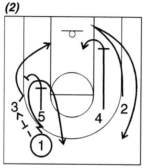

3. On pass to 1, 4 posts, 2 opens up on wing and 5 screens 3 who executes shuffle cut over or under 5 into lane. 1 can pass to 3 cutting or swing ball to 2 who has a better angle. They both have option of passing to 4; also, 1 can beckon 5 to pick in two-man game. 1 or 2 also can penetrate.

4. On pass to 2 by 1, 3 has option to backpick 5's defender or to cut to ballside corner beneath 4. Again, each perimeter player can penetrate. Look for opportunities to pass inside to attack defense. If it collapses or traps, look for inside, outside and over options.

5. As 1 enters ball to 3 on wing, strongside high post man breaks low and to the strongside corner and weakside high post man replaces 5. 2 fakes his defender down and breaks up behind the three-point line. 1 follows his pass for a handback from 3. If defense will not permit 1 access for handback he and 3 reverse roles.

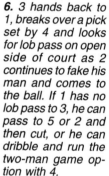

6. 3 hands back to 1, breaks over a pick set by 4 and looks for lob pass on open side of court as 2 continues to fake his man and comes to the ball. If 1 has no lob pass to 3, he can pass to 5 or 2 and then cut, or he can dribble and run the two-man game option with 4.

7. On pass from 1 to 5, 1 uses 4 and cuts to goal around or inside 4 in a give-and-go option. Here we show lob pass option after handback. 5 can also make pass to 3 coming back across lane to strongside low post.

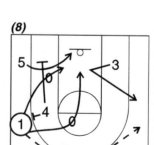

8. On pass to 2, 1 uses screen by 4 and makes a shuffle cut over or under 4 as ball is reversed. After cut by 1, 4 can follow cutter or turn and screen away for 5 in corner. 2 and 3 have option to shoot or penetrate if they feel they have an opening.

Selected Plays for the Box Offense

1. 2 and 3 crossing from weak side with ball above free-throw line on opposite side of court. As 1 enters this area, 4 pins down and sets a double pick in lane with 5 for 2 coming low on baseline; 3 breaks diagonally high to ball in pinch post or screening position to work with 1. On pass from 1 to 2 in corner, 5 comes back to ball on the low post around 4. After his pass to 2, 1 cuts or screens.

2. If 1 uses screen by 3 or a pinch post, he penetrates or brings ball to other side of court. 5 screens 4's defender as 4 comes to ball on low post. 3 steps back, cuts or changes on the weak side with 2.

3. Misdirection double high post screen-and-roll and double screens for post men: 5 and then 4 set high post screens for 1; 1 may bring ball across court or penetrate on either screen. 2 moves along baseline parallel to 1 and 3 goes across lane away from ball to screen for 5 circling to ball. 2 crosses lane, pivots back and sets another baseline screen for 5. 1 drives or looks to 5 on the post.

4. 2 and 3 continue across and up lane and set a staggered double backpick for 4. 4 cuts over or under depending on how defense plays. 2 steps out. 3 looks to circle to an open area as outlet on a switch.

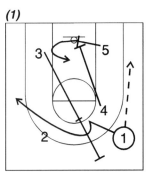

(1)

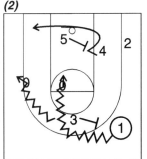

(2)

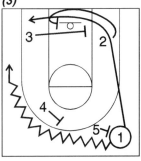

(3)

(4)

(5)

(6)

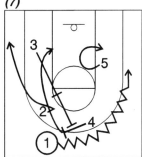

(7)

(8)

Ball movement vs. low post trap by defense: It's the responsibility of the players off the ball to set viable passing lanes for the trapped player.

5. 1 passes ball to 5 on low post, cuts to basket and to other side of the court. His defender or another perimeter defender traps ball on low post. Offensive perimeter players must rotate to ball to give 5 passing options. 5 should pivot on his inside foot to face the defense. He shouldn't try to dribble against the trap unless he wants to stretch it to the corner or wing. Facing gives him vision and confidence.

Diagram No. 6 is handled the same way even though this time the cutter on the pass is 2.

7. High screen-and-roll entry to post 5 as 3 on the weakside low post backpicks the shooter who goes over the top or fades to the weakside corner. 3 steps out to center field after his screen.

8. 1 has ball on the wing. He can pass inside to 5 and then cut, scissor or pick away or 4 can come to the high post area for the high-low option if 5 is fronted or overplayed on the baseline side. The other perimeter players cut, screen, replace or spot up.

Selected Plays for the Box Offense

1. High screen-and-roll, isolation double staggered screen-and-curl: 1 enters the ball to the wing using a high screen set by 4. He has an immediate isolation opportunity if 2's defender follows 2 across the lane and also any of our two-man game options. If 1 passes to 4 stepping back we're in position to reverse the ball to 2 coming off a staggered pick by 3 and 5. 2 can curl off the double if he feels he's open. 4 looks to step in.

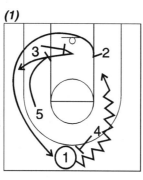

2. High screen-and-roll, clear out and circle back with low post stepping in after curl: 1 enters with or without a high screen by 5 and looks to go one-on-one or for 2 curling back to the middle off 4. If defense switches inside, 4 steps in for the ball on a pass from 1 or 5. If 5 has ball, we have option to reverse ball to 3.

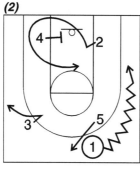

3. 1 enters ball to 3 coming to the wing area and 1 screens away to free the weakside high post coming to the ball. 1 sets a screen and clears out. 3 passes to 4 then sets a double staggered screen with 5 for 2 cutting across the baseline from the weakside block. 4 looks for 2 or he can reverse the ball to 1.

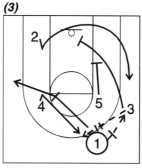

4. On the pass to 2, he can shoot, penetrate, look inside to 5 on the low post or to the middle of the court where 4 loops to the basket using a backpick from 1. **Option:** 2 passing to 1 stepping out so we can again reverse the ball and look inside.

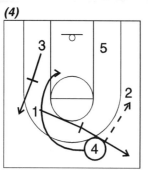

5. Staggered double, clearout, low post and 2-man game options: 1 enters the wing area and passes back to 5 stepping out on the high post. 5 passes to 3 on the weak side and with 1, who hesitated a count, they set a staggered double screen for 2 who has just come off a low pick in the lane from 4. 3 can now work with 4 inside, penetrate and/or look for 2 coming off the screen. 1 clears to either corner and both big men post.

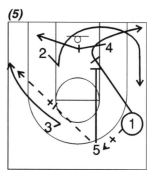

6. 3 has the ball with all scoring and penetrating options available. 4 also is able to post or come up to screen in the two-man game.

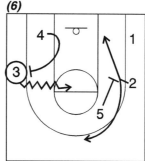

7. Misdirection to post a big man, ISO the point and/or create a double screen for a shooter: 1 penetrates the wing area as 5 screens away and 2 clears across the lane, and in conjunction with 3, backpicks 4, the weakside high post man. 1 has an "ISO" opportunity, a low post pass to 4 coming to the ball or a pass to 3 stepping out after he screens. 3 can then reverse the ball to look for our inside options.

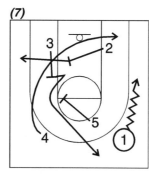

8. ISO, triple screen for shooter and low post option of pick-the-picker: On the screens away as the ball is entered, 2 fakes baseline, 3 screens 4 and steps out and we are in our 1-2-2 or high post offensive setup with many options.

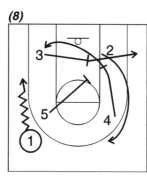

Selected Plays for the Box Offense

Set play with continuity options

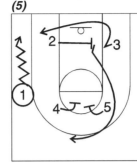

1. Dribble penetration to wing with or without screen. 3 sets misdirection backpick for 2 across lane; 4 and 5 move to weakside lane to set double staggered screen for 2. 1's options: penetrate, pass to 3 posting on switch or pass to 2 at top of the circle.

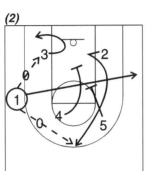

2. Option passes to 2 and 3: On either pass, 1 can screen for player he didn't pass to or cut through middle to weak side looking for return pass, screen one of the big men defenders or spot up in case ball is reversed. We like our big men away from ball to cross or screen each other for rebound position. To start, 3 fakes across and comes back; 2 fakes to ball and uses double screen to set for a shot.

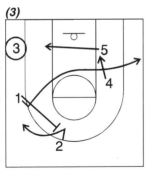

3. 3 steps to corner for ball which opens court for him to penetrate or shoot and gives 4 or 5 opportunities to break to the open low post. 1 cuts and/or screens away for 2. 3 may pass to 2. We have balance, rebounding position and high-percentage shot opportunities as well as penetration and ball reversal options.

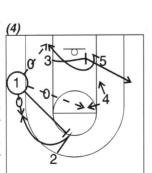

4. 3 may reverse pivot from low post and set horizontal or diagonal screen across on a helping big man defender causing a small-to-big switch. Begin with 2 or 3 in either low post spot.

Same play with different movement

5. Ball has been penetrated on the wing; 2 screens across for 3 as 4 and 5 come together above free-throw line or circle to set a double screen for 2 who has continued up after screening. Remember, 2 can fake across and 3 can come up and use the double screen, too. The player using the pick can split the screeners or come up inside, rather than outside the screen.

6. 2 has option, after setting screen across for 3, to set backpick on 5's defender before he steps out to receive ball. 1 and other players have same options they had in previous play.

7. Once 2 receives ball in center field, he looks for his shot. If it isn't available, 5 has option to come back and set a two-man game screen for 2 who has an open side of the court to work with. If 4 is open, he can cut to the low post or screen away for 3 curling to the ball. 5 rolls or steps back depending on defense. A screen-and-roll is more effective if low post is not cluttered.

8. 4 breaks to low post and/or screens away for 3. If 4 executes the cut to the ballside block, 5 steps back or screens away for 3. 1 and 3 have interchange option at all times.

Selected Plays for the Box Offense
Options to go with plays from the previous page

1. *3 and 5 set a double screen at circle as 2 screens 4 (or 4 backscreens 2) across low post on dribble penetration by 1. The 2-4 action, if switched, gives us a mismatch inside. At the same time, 5 screens down to free 3 popping out (or 3 can backpick 5 and then pop out). 1 can now pass to 4 on the post or 3 who can shoot, pass inside, penetrate, or reverse ball to 2 who has stepped out to the weakside wing.*

2. *We now we can post 5 or 2, our primary shooter, has scoring options. 3 can cut and/or screen away and interchange with 1. We also have inside big man screen away and comeback options.*

3. *2 steps out to the ballside corner or the wing for the entry pass. On the double staggered screen, 3 has the option to cut across the baseline or come high off the double. On either, 1 cuts through and out to the weak side.*

4. *On the pass to 2 in the corner, 1 cuts away and 5 screens 4 cutting to the low post on the strong side. It's important and valuable for individual players to set successive screens on the same play. This move is very difficult to defend.*

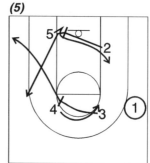

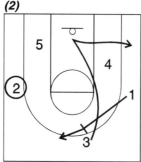

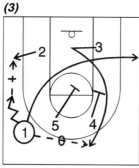

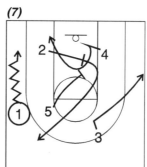

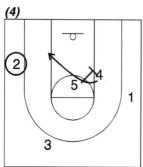

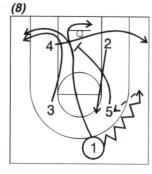

5. *As 1 enters the ball, 2 and 3 screen horizontally across the lane for 5 and 4 then both 2 and 3 cross and cut without screening to different spots on the weak side. We can pass to 5 on the low post, 4 on the elbow for a shot or high-low entry, and we can run a 1-4 two-man game or reverse the ball to our weakside shooters.*

6. Zipper entry combined with a triple post optional diagonal small-to-big downscreen and pick away: *Point must pick his own man if defense tries to switch to keep the big man home to defend and help inside by having 1's defender shoot the gap. We look to post 5 or hit 4 in the lane.*

7. *Triangle action after small-to-big screen across as 3 fades to the weakside corner for a skip pass if the defense tries to double or switch 2 and 3. 5 screening away diagonally gives good screening angles if 2 hesitates before breaking to the top for the ball. We also have good spacing if defense tries to double-team or trap the low post player.*

8. Zipper entry to 2 off screen by 5: *At the same time, 3 fakes downscreening 4's defender, stops, then changes speeds to break to the strongside corner. 2 is isolated on top where he can shoot, run the pinch post or the two-man game with 4. 3 and 1 have options to cross and go to same or opposite corners.*

Selected Plays for the Box Offense
UCLA entry options

1. Point enters ball to weakside post stepping out then 1 cuts inside or outside 5, the strongside high post, to the baseline to set a screen for 2. 5 waits to see which low post man 1 is screening and sets a staggered screen for the same man. (On a special signal, post can screen away and opposite 1.) 2 pops out to the wing after screen and gets pass from 4 as 1 clears to weak side. On an overplay, 2 can cut baseline off 3.

2. 2 has ball and 4 screens down for 3 after making pass. 3 may cut up the lane in zipper move or to strongside corner off screen by 5 on low post. 1 reads 3's cut and moves accordingly. 2 can penetrate.

3. 1 makes entry pass to 3 coming out to the wing and cuts vertically off 4 on high post. 4 waits one count then sets vertical screen for 2 coming to ballside corner after 2 and 5 have set double staggered screen for 1 cutting from ball to weak side.

4. 3 has ball on the wing and we can see his options. 5 can step toward defender, bring him into the lane then come vertically up the lane for pinch post option. Fake and cut give 5 freedom to receive the ball without defensive pressure, important in successfully executing the pinch post.

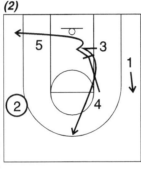

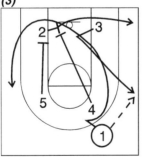

5. Double screen for point man after his initial cut: Used after we have run normal UCLA option with 2-1 pindown. 2's first option is pass to 1 on the cut. Then he looks for his own opportunity to score.

6. 1 hesitates on the baseline. As 2 passes to 5, 1 fakes to strongside corner and cuts baseline to weakside corner area where 3 and 4 set double screen for him coming across and out. 5 looks for 2, but if defense switches out, 3 steps to ball and into the lane.

7. Dribble penetration by 1 to the wing as 4 backpicks 2 on high post then continues to set two-man game screen for 1. If defense forces 1 to sideline, he looks to penetrate to the goal. If 1 dribbles to middle, 3 and 5 set a double screen for 2 coming across the lane as 1 brings ball to him. On a switch, 3 steps in for ball. If 3 isn't free, he continues to weakside corner and 1 either passes to 2, 4 on the roll or 5 inside on low post.

8. If 1 continues his dribble, 5 can diagonally backpick 4 in the lane. This creates a great angle for 2 to hit 4 in the low post on a cut difficult to defend.

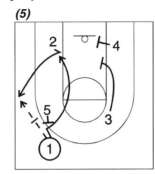

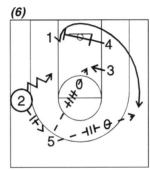

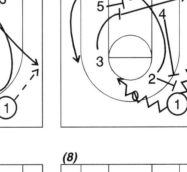

Selected Plays for the Box Offense
Zipper backscreen entry with continuity

1. *4 backpicks 2 on the ball side as 3 and 5 set a double screen on the weakside baseline. 4 continues to the wing to set a two-man game screen for 1 who has used a crossover dribble to penetrate toward the middle, or to pass to 2 off the double screen on the baseline.*

2. *5 and 3 continue across the lane and up towards 4 to set a double backpick on 4's defender.*
***4 must read the double screen's defenders as he cuts over or under to the ballside block. 3 continues out and after 1 passes to 2, 3 interchanges off the ball on the weak side with 1. Interchange can be an upblock or a downscreen. 1 or 3 has the option to cut inside down the lane and to the ball any time they see a defender turn his head or go to trap.*

3. *1 enters by passing to the strongside high post then cuts outside 4's shoulder to the strongside block where he sets a double screen with*

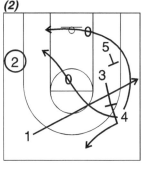

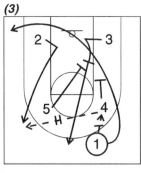

5, the weakside high post man for 2 who is waiting on the baseline. When 5 vacates his area, 2 breaks high to receive a pass from 4. If overplayed, 2 can come up, pull the string and cut backdoor to the goal. 3 has the option to use a double screen, a single screen by 4 to cut baseline to the ball or to center field for a pass coming from 2.

4. *2 passes to 1 who has reversed back to the top of the circle using screens by 5 and 4 as 2 and 3 execute any of our weakside exchange moves.*

5. *If 1 passes to 3 instead of looking inside, 3 can penetrate and 2 can spot in the corner or cross the lane and look to screen one of 4's or 5's inside defenders.*

6. *Continuity with 3 in control on the wing. He can pass inside to 5, look to 2 cutting to an open area from the weak side or drive to the basket to score or draw the defense to him.*

Coach's Edge
Once players understand that effective spacing makes trapping or double-teaming your offense much more difficult for the defense, your movement and execution will improve tremendously.

Selected Plays for the Box Offense

Quick-Hitting Entries vs. Pressure

1. Entry pass to 5 on the high post as 2 clears diagonally across court to strongside wing. 2's cut clears area for 1 who uses back-screen from 4 for lob pass, post up option or fade to weakside sideline. If 1 fades, 5 can drive, shoot, post 3, pass to 2 or 4 and then cut.

2. On skip or flare pass to 1, 2 then 3, set double stag-gered backpick for 5. This sets up lob to 5 and allows 1 a one-on-one option. 4 can pick 1 in our two-man game, but here he screens away on 2 then 3 in pick-the-picker op-tion. If 1 has no lob to 5 he can look to post 5 on low post.

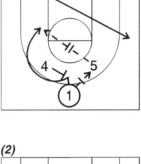

UCLA entry

3. With our wings on high post to set up weakside low post duck-in or 1-3 back-screen option 1 pas-ses to 3 popping out and waits for upblock from 5 coming to high post. 1 rubs his man off the pick and looks for return pass from 3. If no pass is made, 1 waits on baseline between lane and 3-point line. 2 fans out to clear and spot up.

4. 3 passes to 5 step-ping out. As 5 gets ball, 4 fakes towards 2 and ducks into lane to seal his defender and look for pass from 5. If 4 is fronted he can reverse pivot on his man, clear out or backpick for 2. 5's other option is 1-3 backpick, or pindown and ball reversal to 2.

Entries vs. Extreme Point Guard Defensive Pressure with Help

5. As 1 passes to 4 on high post, both 2 and 3 break to wings and 5 backpicks 1's de-fender. 1 fakes flare and circles off screen into the lane. If he isn't free he can backpick 2's defender on the wing. Now 5 can pass to 2 or 1 or reverse ball to 3 to open the court for movement and pass and cut op-tions.

6. Second option for 1 on high post entry in this series has 1 fak-ing screen away for 4 and instead curling back around him to make high post de-fender help deny 1 the return pass. This en-ables 4 to slash into the lane for a pass from 5 as 2 and 3 break to the wings causing defenders to follow them.

7. Low post positions break out to wings to establish 1-4 align-ment to combat pres-sure. 1 dribbles in one direction and on a pre-determined signal (i.e. reverse dribble), weakside high post man reverse pivots into now vacant free-throw lane. If the point can't reverse or cross over, he still has two-man game option with 5 or UCLA entry to wing.

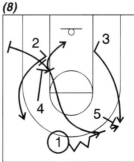

8. Wing pass entry with double staggered vertical downscreen to weak side to set up a 3-5 two-man game or clearout option for the wing. Double screen is to free the shooter coming from low post and point cuts to weakside cor-ner. Post man breaks to low post after they screen down for shooter.

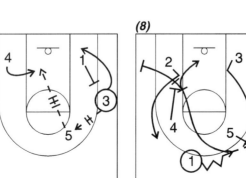

Selected Plays for the Box Offense

Clearout options for the weakside high post position

"Special Need" or "Final-Shot-in-the-Game" Play

1. Dribble entry to the wing as shooter clears baseline to ball off low post screen which sets up a reverse pivot lob opportunity for the high post. If 4 isn't free he can continue down lane to low post where we have option to pass to 5 and permit him to pass to 4 if 4 has been able to duck in and seal his defender. We also have strongside scissor or curl options available.

2. Weakside high post clearout on entry pass with high post flare away as shooter on baseline clears out across lane. If 4 can't take defender one-on-one he can look for 2-3 curl or step in on defensive switch near the goal. We can also clear 2 to the corner and look to pass to 5 as he dives diagonally down lane to basket.

3. High screen-and-roll entry to permit pass to wing breaking out. Passer picks away with weakside high post to set up low post curl to ball. We try to force low post defender to fight through two screens, instead of one. Entry pass also gives immediate "iso" option to wing.

4. Screen down zipper curl and clearout with weakside backpick enables us to isolate low post area as we take away defensive help. 2 and 3 are outlets on perimeter vs. low post double-team.

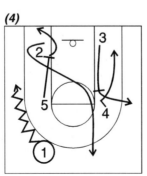

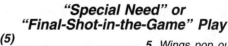

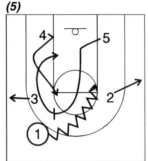

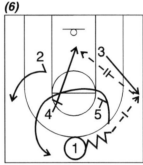

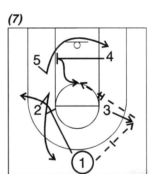

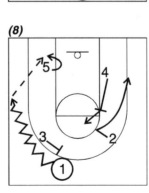

5. Wings pop out to corners to spot up and weakside low post breaks high to set up two-man game or give point man opportunity to penetrate. Shooters are positioned for penetration and pitch vs. double-team or help and post man is in position to step out or roll to basket. Some teams also have weakside low post set a backpick for the high post after dribbler penetrates past screener.

6. Point entry pass to wing vs. a team denying point a return pass. Point cuts around and under two high post short downscreens and second high post screener slashes to basket from weak side when his defender tries to body check or help out on the cutter. Weakside low post shooter breaks to an open area.

7. Wing players set up in high post positions. On entry pass to one wing, point screens away for a shooter as the low post man on ball side screens across and pivots back to ball in opposite direction of cutter. 3 should try to dribble down for a better passing angle.

8. We post the big man on the block after two-man game using wing entry. 3 may or may not set screen for 1. Backpicking by 4 on 2's defender on weak side makes play effective because 4's defender must worry about 4 stepping to ball and into lane. The weakside flare is difficult to defend when properly executed.

Selected Plays for the Box Offense

1. *1 - 4 high post backdoor entry vs. wing overplay. Options: No backdoor pass means cutter must clear out around double pick downscreen by 5 and 3. This enables 4 to take his defender one-on-one or 3 to cut off 5's back after they set the screen for 2. Especially effective against 2-3 defensive switch.*

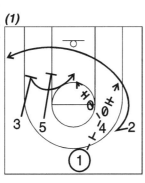

2. *Wing entry to "ISO" 2 as 1, 4 and 5 move away to screen and free 3 from the weakside low post. 1 fakes the screen and cuts through to the weak side looking for the ball. This is a misdirection screen for 5 that comes from an unexpected area of the court.*

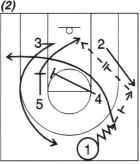

3. *Dribble penetration and pass to wing by 1 as 2 clears away across lane around double screen on weak side from 4 and 5. 1 also can keep dribble alive to penetrate or pass back to 2 coming off double screen. On pass to 3, 1 cuts away, 4 continues to low post. We again have multiple options on one play.*

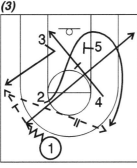

4. *High post entry with a flare way which again sets up isolation from high post as player on low post and other high post player screen down on weakside low post position. Low post player fakes a screen and curls back into lane for ball.*

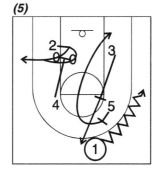

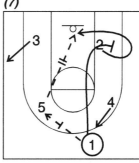

5. Misdirection double screen off continuity: *Dribble penetration to wing with zipper backpick from low post. First option is to the cutter (5); second option is to screener (3) above the circle. If point keeps dribble alive he can run two-man game with 3. If dribble is not live, he can run a handoff with 3 or 3 can dribble the ball to other side of the court where 4 pins down on 2.*

6. *As ball is brought across the court, dribbler can penetrate to goal and 4 and 2 go across the court to screen for 5 who is coming to the ball. This is our pick-the-picker action to the low post as other players move, spot up and continue to screen for one another.*

7. *High post misdirection backpick for the wing. 1 cuts vertically down the lane after his high post entry pass. 5 can penetrate, pass and/or fake to 3 on the wing. This enables 1 to set a backpick on 2, the weakside wing who is being pressured and denied the ball.*

8. *Similar to previous play. Point enters to high post and flares away from ball to interchange with 3 on weakside wing. First option is weakside high post dive into the lane. Second is one-on-one penetration to the left from high post; third option is 4 backpicking strongside wing who is being overplayed. Cutters always have option to go over or under backpicks.*

165

Objectives of a Successful Offensive Play

1. Obtain a good shot for a good shooter in a comfortable area and position on the court.

2. Big and small men in triangles with weakside and defensive balance positions should the shooter miss.

3. Make players aware of each other's strengths and tendencies.

4. Players must be aware of where most offensive rebounds land or bounce so we have a better chance of grabbing them and converting easy scores.

5. Make shooters aware that they are the most dangerous offensive rebounders because they know where the missed shot is going to land.

6. Ability to penetrate the defense.

7. Options should the defense stop our initial move.

8. Coach's awareness of and his ability to take advantage of his players' skills when constructing plays.

10
Basketball Scouting

Scouting is important in the development of an offensive attack. Previously we mentioned how critical it is to continually refine and fine tune the offense as the season progresses. A method that permits us to best accomplish this task is to have a former player, coach or knowledgeable associate not directly connected to our program scout our team.

These individuals scout a preseason scrimmage, exhibition game or our first regular season game and submit reports after compiling their data. This helps us prepare for our season and make adjustments in playing style or tactics. They scout us in the same manner as would one of our future opponents. We all need an objective analysis and evaluation of our work, and a person not with us each practice can best provide this information.

We also have them periodically scout us during the season and again prior to the playoffs. Adjustments are made, and team and individual styles of play change as the season progresses that might not have been recognized otherwise.

We want to anticipate and be one step ahead of the opposition. We want to know things about our style of coaching and our players' performances that only someone not directly involved can provide. They can tell us who they'd concentrate on stopping and who they would make beat them if they were facing us.

Robert Kennedy once said, "Strong men criticize themselves." Self-evaluation is a great way to improve performance and productivity. Staff, team and individual team members spend countless hours reviewing video during a season to help us judge performances and prepare for future opponents.

We believe in scouting. We prefer to have more than one recent written report and video of each opponent before playing them. Scouting is scientific and the amount of time a coach devotes to it depends on his philosophy. If it wasn't important in today's changing technological society, however, why would so many corporations, professionals and businesses devote countless hours developing specialized programs that use computers and videos in training and preparation? It requires effort, but the results speak for themselves. Not all of us are blessed with a Michael Jordan, Larry Bird or Magic Johnson to turn to when things are difficult.

A number of years ago, I worked with Ed Krinsky, now vice president and general manager of the United States Basketball League's Long Island Surf, to develop an outline for basketball scouting which covered all of the information we needed to know about future opponents. It's refined annually to keep abreast of changes in the game. It's included here because we feel it might prove beneficial for future game preparation. Charts can be developed based on individual needs and preferences, but we recommend diagramming all of an opponent's offensive and defensive sets and out-of-bounds plays. We urge scouts to include any information that will help prepare the game plan.

Each coach can decide what to use or disregard, but these are the things we think are important in evaluating ourselves or a future opponent.

Note: Whenever possible, ascertain the verbal or hand signals or keys used to call specific offensive plays or defensive alignments.

I. Individual Characteristics
    A. Shooting
        1. Who is primary scorer, from where is he most effective and how do they get him the ball
        2. Most dangerous shooters
        3. Range of all shooters
        4. Who do they look to who can shoot dependably under pressure
        5. Best and poorest free-throw shooters
        6. Starters, frontline reserves, game statistics, heights, weights
        7. Who substitutes for whom and do roles change when substitutes enter the game
    B. Ballhandling
        1. Who handles the ball under pressure
        2. Who can we pressure most effectively
        3. Who are their best feeders
    C. Offensive Moves
        1. Who can drive and penetrate
        2. Is there anyone who can only can go one way
        3. Who can shoot, drive and pass off the dribble
        4. Which way do the post men turn
        5. Which players stop for the jump shot

D. Rebounding
   1. Three most dangerous rebounders
   2. Is there someone who doesn't go to the board or leaks out on a shot or pass inside
   3. Do they tip the ball out to the foul line or a specific area or do they always bring it down

E. Speed and Conditioning
   1. Speed and quickness of each player
   2. Does anyone tire easily because he is not in shape

II. Basic defense
   A. Man-to-man or zone
      1. Can we fast-break and beat them down the floor
      2. Where do they begin to pick up
      3. Where do they apply pressure if at all
      4. Do they try to force or direct the ball to the middle, sideline or baseline
      5. Will they try to help out or switch; when switching do they do it to force action or help. Do they switch on all crosses with and without the ball and on equals and unequals
      6. How will they play the post
      7. Is anyone prone to fouling and getting into foul trouble
      8. Do they block out
      9. Where should we direct our attack, weakness to exploit
      10. Do they trap, double-team, rotate and help. When, where and how
      11. Which players tend to help out the most

   B. Combination
      1. Answer all of the same questions you would for Man-to-Man or Zone
      2. How do they play the cut towards the ball
      3. How do they play the cut away from the ball
      4. Who covers the flash and high post
      5. Do they trap, double-team, rotate and help. When, where and how

   C. Zone
      1. Can we fast-break and beat them down the court
      2. Can we score and exploit them by going to the strong side

3. Can and should we reverse the ball

4. Can we get the ball into the middle

5. What areas are they slow to cover

6. Are they vulnerable to attack from behind

7. Do they trap, double-team, rotate and help. When, where and how

III. Basic Offense

    A. Patterns and Tendencies

        1. How does the team set up in the frontcourt

        2. Individual set plays and/or continuity of motion

        3. What plays do they run most frequently

        4. Are they looking to set up a particular player

        5. Which side of the floor do they favor

        6. Do they have a weakside attack

        7. How deliberate is their offense. Do they score quickly or "milk" the shot clock

        8. Who do they look for and what do they do in a need or special situation

        9. What will be our best suggested defensive matchup

      10. Explain their zone offense and principal threats

    B. Fast Break

        1. To what extent do they look to run

        2. Do they use the sideline or middle fast break

        3. Do they have a set pattern or do they just try to fill the lanes

        4. Do the wing men cross on the baseline, fade, etc.

        5. Will they take the jump shot, from where

        6. Where are their outlets

        7. Can we pressure the rebounder's outlet pass

        8. Do they run from a free throw

        9. Do they have a transition and or secondary break. Explain

      10. Do they release or leak a man downcourt early

      11. Do the center and other big men try to beat their opponents down the court

IV. Special or Need Situations

    A. Out-of-bounds

        1. Do they try to score or just inbound safely

      2. Do they have a specific setup or does it vary

      3. Are they looking for a particular player; do they have options and continuity

      4. What is their last-second out-of-bounds play

      5. Diagram every sideline and under-the-basket out-of-bounds play

  B. Jump Ball

      1. Do they try to score or just get possession

      2. Where do they tip; to a specific player

  C. Pressing Defense

      1. Man-to-man, zone or combination

      2. Full-, three-quarter- or half-court. Explain

      3. Where do they try to double-team and trap

      4. Where are their weaknesses

      5. How often and when do they normally press

  D. Press Offense

      1. Who handles the ball

      2. Do they have a pattern

      3. Who comes down the floor

      4. Do they post up in the middle

      5. Do they look to fast break and score or simply set up after crossing half-court

      6. Do they utilize the long pass

      7. Where are they most vulnerable

      8. Should we zone or man-to-man press them

  E. Freeze, Stall or Delay Game

      1. Do they have one

      2. When do they go into it

      3. Are they looking to score

      4. Do they have continuity. Explain

Emphasize these basic points in the scouting summation:

- What are the opponent's strengths and weaknesses?
- What do they do that will give us trouble?
- How can we utilize our personnel most effectively?

- If they fast break, are they the type of team that successfully converts a great percentage of their fastbreak opportunities?

- What do we need to do to beat them?

- What are their pet plays and moves?

- What do they do after time-outs? Change defenses? Always run a play?

- Do they make adjustments during the game? When and how?

The report should include the game program and a copy of the official final and halftime game statistics.

Coach's Edge
Some teams like to move and reverse the ball, get a good shot and make it. Other teams simply like to reverse the ball, get a bad shot and make it. We like to know which team we are playing against.

Statistical Keys to Winning Offensive Basketball

Most coaches and players run to view the "stats" as soon as the game or first half is over. We all have a tendency to evaluate our performances based on the statistics. While this provides a certain measure of individual and team consistency and performance, it isn't entirely indicative in evaluating championship team basketball.

We have a list of things which more accurately determine game performance as a team. We chart each area every game and then review them with our players whenever we dissect our performance.

The areas we are most concerned with when evaluating offensive performance are:

1. Did we shoot more free throws and have a higher free-throw percentage than our opponents?

2. Did we have more offensive rebounds and putback baskets?

3. Was our number of offensive opportunities greater than our opponents, and was our ratio of turnovers-to-attempts lower?

4. Did we have more assists than they did during the game and what was our ratio of turnovers to assists?

5. We'd like a better field-goal percentage, but we understand that would depend on the type of shot opportunities we had.

6. We want more three-point play opportunities (fouls in the act of shooting) and more completed three-point plays than the opposition.

7. Three-point shots: Did we shoot a greater percentage than the opposition and make at least 38 to 40 percent of our shots from beyond the three-point line?

8. We want to shoot and make more layups and shots in the paint (higher percentage field-goal attempts).

9. How many times did we pass the ball inside? To whom? How many times did the inside person pass the ball back outside? We like to know how many times it went in, out and in again because this is a fine offensive weapon.

10. How many fast-break chances did we have in each half and how many points did we score on the break? What is our percentage of success in this area compared to our opponents?

Set goals in each of these areas. Compare and evaluate your performance each game and season.

Coach's Edge

Work hard at being consistent. If you are consistent, you know what to expect and how to adjust. Inconsistent teams may win some games, but it's more likely that they will not be able to sustain the effort and concentration required to be a winner every night.

About the Author

Herb Brown is a 35-year basketball coaching veteran. He is currently an assistant coach for the Indiana Pacers. A seven-time coach of the year with more than 700 victories, his teams have won championships on the professional, international and college levels. A highly regarded and respected clinician and lecturer, Brown has written numerous articles on basketball in the United States and Europe.

Herb Brown

Brown's teams have always been classified as over-achievers. Since 1973 when he joined the professional coaching ranks, only one of his teams has failed to qualify for postseason playoff competition. Most advanced past the first round. Two of Brown's teams won championships in the first year of a league's existence (Western Basketball Association and European Professional Basketball League), and both of his CBA expansion teams won division titles (Puerto Rico and Cincinnati) in the first year. Although his teams are known for outstanding defense, Brown is a proponent of the fast break and multiple offense.

Brown led the Detroit Pistons to two consecutive playoff appearances while a head coach. The 1975-76 team was in last place when he took over as head coach. It not only made the playoffs, but also became the first Piston team to ever advance past the first round in NBA postseason competition.

In six seasons of coaching in the ACB, Spain's highest professional league, his teams have never failed to make the playoffs and have reached the league semifinals three times. In one Korac Cup European playoff competition, they reached the semifinals before being eliminated. In their other four appearances they advanced to the quarter-finals.

The results in Puerto Rico were the same. His teams advanced to the league semifinals six times and won the championship in their only trip to the finals, upsetting the regular-season league champion. Only one of his squads failed to qualify for postseason competition during his 15-year tenure as a coach on the island.

Many of his former college and professional players have gone on to outstanding NBA, CBA, college and international coaching careers. He has the added distinction of having coached a number of players to MVP honors in their respective leagues.

He also has been a European scout for the Indiana Pacers and Chicago Bulls.

You'll be right in the game with these new basketball books from Masters Press!

Holding Court: What's Wrong with Sports and How to Fix It

by Dick Vitale with Dick Weiss

When Dick Vitale speaks out, sports fans listen. And speak out he does in this insightful new book, on everything from the baseball strike to the Simpson trial. As one of America's leading basketball analysts, Vitale concentrates especially on the sport he knows best and looks at the game from every angle. How has coaching changed? Who are the best coaches and what makes them great? Has the increased emphasis on academics made a difference? Vitale looks at these and a host of other subjects including the return of Michael Jordan, television's impact on college basketball, and, of course, the NCAA tournament.

$22.95 • 256 pages • 6 x 9 • B&W Photos • Hardback • ISBN: 1-57028-037-1

ACC Basketball

by Peter C. Bjarkman

From its birth in 1954, the Atlantic Coast Conference rapidly ascended to become the centerpiece of college basketball. No other conference has won more NCAA tournament games or boasts a higher postseason winning percentage. With storied players such as Michael Jordan and coaches like Dean Smith, an ACC team has been among the NCAA's Final Four 22 times since the conference was formed. A follow-up to Bjarkman's *Big Ten Basketball, ACC Basketball* contains school-by-school team histories and stats, all-time great coaches and players, a look at some of the conference's most memorable moments, all-time team selection and a trivia section.

$14.95 • 256 pages • 7 3/8 x 9 1/4 • B&W Photos • Paper
ISBN: 1-57028-038-X

Basketball's Balanced Offense

by Jim Harrick

Author Jim Harrick, coach of the 1995 NCAA champion UCLA Bruins, gives a detailed explanation of the offense developed by Ward "Piggy" Lambert and perfected by coaching legend John Wooden. With the aid of numerous diagrams to illustrate the various plays, Harrick goes through the offense step-by-step. A section on drills is included as are chapters on running the offense from the low post and the 1-2-2 set.

$12.95 • 192 pages • 7 x 10 • B&W Photos & Diagrams • Paper
ISBN: 1-57028-023-1

All of our books are available at better bookstores or by calling Masters Press at (800) 722-2677. Catalogs available upon request.